CHRISTIAN ENCOUNTERS

SERGEANT YORK

CHRISTIAN ENCOUNTERS

SERGEANT
YORK

JOHN PERRY

THOMAS NELSON
Since 1798

NASHVILLE   DALLAS   MEXICO CITY   RIO DE JANEIRO

© 2010 by John Perry

Published in Nashville, Tennessee. Thomas Nelson is a registered trademark of
Thomas Nelson, Inc.

Thomas Nelson, Inc., titles may be purchased in bulk for educational, business,
fund-raising, or sales promotional use. For information, please e-mail
SpecialMarkets@ThomasNelson.com.

Published in association with the literary agency of Wolgemuth & Associates, Inc.

Scripture quotations are from the King James Version of the Bible (public
domain).

Library of Congress Cataloging-in-Publication Data

Perry, John, 1952–
  Sergeant York / John Perry.
    p. cm. — (Christian encounters)
  Includes bibliographical references.
  ISBN 978-1-59555-025-5
  1. York, Alvin Cullum, 1887–1964. 2. Soldiers—United States—Biography.
  3. World War, 1914–1918—Campaigns—France. 4. United States. Army—
  Biography. I. Title.
  D570.9.Y7P47 2010
  940.4'36—dc22
  [B]   2010028462

Printed in the United States of America

10 11 12 13 HCI 6 5 4 3 2 1

CONTENTS

INTRODUCTION

Writing about history, I generally spend a lot of time shuffling through old letters and digging (often literally) through stacks and boxes of musty documents. The story of Sergeant Alvin York is different in that, in addition to all the usual research, I have had the pleasure of speaking with friends, neighbors, and family members who knew the man. Archival documents, wonderful as they are, can't explain themselves or answer a question. Having this living link with my subject provides a rare level of comfort in stating facts and drawing conclusions.

Not that the story of Alvin York is cut-and-dried. Like anyone with strongly felt opinions, York had his enemies. And he was unflinchingly partisan when it came to politics: in line with most Southern voters of the time, he was a Yellow Dog Democrat who considered Hoover a buffoon and FDR the nation's savior. He was more a doer than a thinker, a man of action whose energy and resolve led him to jump into situations he hadn't fully thought through, sometimes to troublesome effect.

York never went looking for fame or wealth. They came to him, and he handled them as best he could. The fact that he single-handedly captured 132 Germans and killed maybe two dozen would be unbelievable if not for the detailed official eye-witness accounts. York thought it was a miracle, and so do I. For decades he resisted cashing in on his celebrity, declaring time and again that "Uncle Sam's uniform ain't for sale." The threat of annihilation on the eve of World War II changed his mind. His desire to see America standing strong against mania-cal threats from Germany and Japan finally outweighed his natural humility and self-imposed standard of propriety.

As the result of the Hollywood blockbuster that carried his name, Sergeant York became a hero all over again and a wealthy man, and gained an informal but significant position of influence in international affairs. Then, in an ironic twist worthy of Greek tragedy, the fame York had avoided for so long and handled with such selfless grace led to hardship and humiliation. Years that should have been filled with honors and accolades were spent struggling merely to survive.

Yet in good times and bad, York was astonishingly con-sistent, upbeat, and gracious. He never crowed of his success and never complained of his ill treatment at the hands of peo-ple who should have known better. His secret—which was no secret at all, because he talked of it for nearly fifty years—was his rock-solid faith in God and in Christ. York's religion was his lodestar, the one infallible and unchanging component in a life filled to overflowing with changes and contrasts: a man with a third-grade education who built a school; a backwoods Tennessee mountaineer who inspired a Hollywood hit; a poor man who died poor but was rich in between; a life that began with plow horses and kerosene lamps but extended into a world of nuclear power and space exploration.

For Alvin York, wherever he was and whatever his circumstances, Jesus was there to comfort, guide, and point the way. From the day his heart was transformed by Christ through a mother's love, York was a Christian soldier of the truest sort. The phrase may sound hokey to twenty-first-century ears, but the honor, diligence, patriotism, and faith they describe remain timeless.

Soli Deo Gloria
John Perry
Nashville
Memorial Day, 2010

1

NEW YEAR'S PROMISE

Alvin York was drunk again. He'd liked the sensation of corn whiskey down his throat ever since he sneaked his first sip as a boy, but he really took to it after his daddy died. Life was hard during the best of times in the Wolf River Valley of Tennessee, and Alvin's life was a struggle even by valley standards. He and his people didn't complain because they had no idea how poor they truly were. Life had always been that way; they were seldom disappointed, because they expected so little. Alvin's family owned seventy-five acres in this beautiful, isolated pocket of farm country seven miles from the Kentucky line. It was just enough to scratch out a living for him, his mother, and eight younger brothers and sisters. Two older brothers were married and on their own, leaving Alvin head of the household.

Days he worked his own land and hired out to help neighboring farmers. Nights he spent at his father's smithy, where he could earn another fifty cents after it was too dark to plow. Some nights after that, he'd go out for a nip.

Folks called him "Big 'Un," and everything he did, he did in a big way. He was big himself, a burly, barrel-chested ox of a man, muscles grown taut and strong from a lifetime of steadying a plow and wielding a hammer. His head was topped with a thick, unruly thatch of red hair. In a time and place where every man was a good shot, his marksmanship was legendary. No one could afford to waste ammunition putting meat on the table, but Alvin's skill was a cut above. He could drop five birds with five rifle shots. He could put two bullets in the same target hole at twenty paces.

When Big 'Un got into a fight, he fought big. Sometimes with his fists, sometimes with a knife—but always in it to win. When he drank, he drank big. Alcohol made him even more of a fighter, so after a night of moonshine whiskey, Alvin was likely to fight anybody on any terms. Like the other men thereabouts, Alvin did his drinking at one of the "blind tigers" near the settlements of Static and Bald Rock. A blind tiger was a ramshackle bar straddling the state line, with a white stripe painted down the middle of the floor. Kentucky was on one side of the room, and Tennessee on the other. Kentucky residents went into Tennessee to drink, and vice versa. When the local sheriff from either side arrived, customers hopped back into their own states, out of jurisdiction of whoever came through the door. Plenty of other popular vices were available there, too, all in one convenient location. Blind tigers were where Alvin and his neighbors did a lot of card playing, scrapping, and cursing.

His father would have been disappointed but not surprised. Alvin had been a handful even as a boy. He hadn't gotten any milder by the time his father lost his life, when Alvin was in his twenties. William York died late in 1911, likely from pneumonia after a mule he was shoeing kicked him in the chest. That loss seemed to make Big 'Un even more boisterous and disruptive. He'd shoot a neighbor's chickens off the fence on his way home from a night of carousing. He made a ruckus outside the Methodist church in the middle of a Sunday service. He got in trouble with the law for fighting and for selling guns somebody said were stolen, though Alvin said they weren't. He never was arrested because there never was enough evidence to bring him in. Maybe it was because people in the Wolf River Valley felt sorry for Mother York and that son of hers who was so hard to handle.

Mary Brooks York was the most mild-mannered, hardworking, God-fearing woman anybody in the community ever knew. She'd been a devoted wife and mother, but nothing she did seemed to make any difference when it came to Alvin. Her father and husband had been responsible, sober family men. Though she'd done what she could to teach her children what was right, Alvin had a mind of his own, and he'd do as he pleased. Without a doubt he loved his mother, yet he couldn't seem to act like she wanted him to. Most men his age were already married and had families of their own. Here he was, at twenty-seven, wild as a billy goat, and likely headed for jail or an early grave. All Mother York could do for her boy was pray. And she prayed hard day after day, year after year.

She was praying on New Year's Eve, 1914, when Alvin was out drinking as usual. As she sat in her rocker, with a few coals still burning in the kitchen fireplace, the soft glow of a kerosene lamp lit the room. The York cabin was simple but comfortable, with a kitchen and eating area separated from the living room, where Mother York's bed also was. The nine children still at home shared a second-story sleeping loft.

At last she heard Alvin's unsteady steps on the front porch and looked up as he opened the door, letting in a blast of icy December wind. As many times as he'd come home like this, she had never waited up for him before. Seeing her sitting there, wrapped in her threadbare shawl, gave him a shock. She stopped rocking as their eyes met. Alvin looked away and stared at the floor, shame working its way through the alcoholic fog.

"When are you going to be a man like your father and grandfather?" she asked softly.

His father's honesty had been legendary in the community, to the point that neighbors called him in to settle their disputes instead of going to court. Alvin had never known his grandfather, but he'd heard about how he had expressed his love for his wife and children to the Confederate vigilantes who killed him. This was Alvin's heritage, men who knew instinctively what was right without having to stew about it. His mother had tried to steer Alvin in that direcion as well, but in the three years since his daddy died, he'd veered ever faster toward a life of ruin.

Hearing his mother's voice, Alvin sensed a strange, unfamiliar feeling. The years of drinking and fighting flashed through his mind. The waste and emptiness of his life stood out as never before. It was like seeing himself clearly for the first time, and what he saw saddened him.

Alvin couldn't speak. His knees gave way. Kneeling beside Mother York's chair, he put his head in her lap; took her bony, rough hand in his massive, calloused one; and started to cry. Through his tears he saw that she was crying too; it was the first time he'd ever seen her weep. He had disappointed his mother. He had disappointed the God she served so faithfully and to whom she prayed so earnestly. He felt his heart being deeply changed.

When he finally found his voice, he said, "Mother, I promise you tonight that I will never drink again as long as I live. I will never smoke or chew again. I will never gamble again. I will never cuss or fight again. I will live the life God wants me to live."

Mother York looked into the face of her boy, his image flickering in the firelight. "I know you will, Son," she said. And so, New Year's Day 1915 marked the beginning of a new life for Alvin York. Recalling the moment years later, he said, "God just took ahold of my life. My little old mother had been praying for me so long, and I guess the Lord finally decided to answer her."[1]

Alvin Cullum York had been born December 13, 1887, in the settlement of Pall Mall, Tennessee, in the Wolf River Valley. The land was hunting ground for generations of Shawnee, Cherokee, Creek, and Chickasaw. The plentiful game attracted tribes as distant as the Iroquois, who came all the way from New York with their hunting bows and skinning knives. By around 1800 the first white settlers moved into the valley from Virginia and the Carolinas, including a twenty-four-year-old homesteader named Coonrod Pile, who bought a tract of land from a Continental Army veteran who'd received it by an act of Congress awarding property to retired soldiers.

Despite the fact that Pile's deed included "a cabin by the name of Livingston's cabin," the legend sprang up that his first shelter was a cave he discovered while gathering firewood to roast a deer.

In 1808 Coonrod was awarded a direct land grant of additional property by the government of Tennessee. Other settlers came to and through the valley as the years passed, including a young man from East Tennessee named David Crockett. "Davy" Crockett (evidently, no one actually called him that) served under Andrew Jackson in the Creek War and had settled with his family on a farm in the valley by 1817. He didn't stay long. Elected to the state legislature in 1821, he later served three terms in the U.S. House of Representatives before heading farther west in search of adventure. Crockett died at the Alamo in 1836, fighting for Texas independence against Mexico.

John Clemens was another settler in Coonrod's day. A Virginia native who came to the county seat of Jamestown—over the hills to the southwest of Pall Mall and the valley—he established a law practice, acquired a lot of land, and became a leading citizen of Fentress County. After a few years he, like Crockett, heard the call of the frontier and left with his pregnant wife for Missouri, where their son, Samuel, was born. The boy never saw Fentress County, but he wrote about it under the world-famous pen name Mark Twain in his satirical novel *The Gilded Age*.

By the time Fentress County was formed in 1823, old Coonrod Pile was one of the most respected men in the region, and one of the wealthiest. He owned tens of thousands of acres, large tracts of standing timber, a general store, a flour mill, and a number of slaves. One reason for his success was that he never produced more of anything than he could use or sell to his neighbors. The terrain and isolation made it too expensive to ship any goods out of the valley except for logs, which he could lash together in rafts and float downriver to Nashville.

Pile's prosperity allowed him to live a life of ease, and he eventually grew so fat he could scarcely walk. Late in life he traveled everywhere in a two-wheeled cart pulled by a pair of oxen.

The only thing in the world he feared was lightning. At the first flash he would waddle to the cave he had discovered years before, outrunning the cart, and sit there cursing until the storm passed.

Coonrod died in 1849, the most powerful and influential man in Fentress County. His riches were split among his eight children. One daughter, Delilah Lucinda, married David Crockett's nephew William. Another, Alvin's ancestor Elijah, had eleven children. Once Elijah divided his one-eighth of the original family fortune eleven ways, each child of the next generation had enough to live on, but they were far from wealthy.

Elijah was too old to fight in the Civil War, yet, like many Tennesseans in the officially Confederate state, he supported the Union. When U.S. general Ambrose Burnside marched his forces through Pall Mall, one of his soldiers was a redhead from Michigan named William Brooks. This Northern cavalryman fell in love with Elijah's daughter, Nancy. The two had been married only about two years and had an infant daughter named Mary Elizabeth when Brooks killed a man after an argument. Brooks was eventually captured and imprisoned, but he never stood trial. A vigilante mob sprung him from jail, shot him, and dragged him behind a horse until he died. A few weeks later, Nancy gave birth to their son, William, whose hair was fiery red like his father's. Nancy, Mary, and the baby moved in with her father, Elijah Pile.

Uriah York was another Union sympathizer from Tennessee, a U.S. Army veteran who'd fought with General Winfield Scott in the Mexican War. He went north to Kentucky to join the Union army, leaving his wife and son, William, behind, but soon he returned with the measles. When a Confederate posse came looking for him, he hid in a canebrake. He eluded his captors, but caught pneumonia and died.

William York and Mary Elizabeth Brooks grew up as neighbors, both of them fatherless children, casualties of a destructive war that set brother against brother. In time their acquaintance ripened into love, and the two were married on Christmas Day 1881, when he was eighteen and she was fifteen. At first they lived in Coonrod Pile's old house with Mary's mother, who had inherited the house and seventy-five acres. Then, when Mary's aunt Polly Pile passed away, Mary inherited her land, and she and William moved over to farm it. The only building on the property was a log corncrib that Elijah Pile had built many years before. William went to work turning it into a family home. He chinked the holes between the logs and laid down a puncheon floor—small logs halved lengthwise with the flat sides facing up. In time he built a second room, a porch, kitchen, and sleeping loft, and put lumber siding over the log exterior.

The Yorks had eleven children in nineteen years; feeding so many mouths was a constant struggle. For his wisdom and fairness in informally settling local disputes, William became known as "Judge York," though he was illiterate and had never spent a day in school. For all his wisdom, he had little resolve when it came to earning a living. He'd rather spend all night hunting with his dogs in the woods than walk all day behind a mule-drawn plow. To supplement his meager income as a farmer, William taught himself blacksmithing and had a steady business in iron and woodworking. Once the two oldest boys, Henry and Joseph, were out of the house, William passed down the craft to his next son, Alvin, and used him as an assistant at the forge.

As a grown man Alvin competed in shooting matches where there were five prizes: four quarters of butchered beef, then a fifth prize of the hide and horns. Sometimes he'd win every round and lead the contest cow home on hoof. So many shooters hit bull's-eyes that the number of center shots alone often wasn't enough to declare a winner. The judge would measure the distance between the center of the rifle ball and the center of the bull's-eye. The fact that Alvin could win every contest of the day with that level of competition was proof even that among superlative marksmen he was unsurpassed.

Shooting competitions honed the hunting skills men and boys used almost every day, in every kind of weather, as they went after meat for the table. Alvin loved hunting, especially night hunting with dogs, from the time he was old enough to carry a gun. Boys in the valley often had a lightweight .22 by the age of ten. Women and girls didn't hunt, but had their own forms of working recreation. Some were informal, like sitting with a neighbor to shell a pot of peas. Others were more organized, such as a quilting bee or circle, where several women gathered in one of the homes to make a quilt together. They spent days cutting the pattern pieces from scrap cloth, then sewed the patterns—a star, a square, a bow, a cluster of octagons—together, then quilted the fabric with cotton batting to make it warm.

Crops and livestock, cooking, canning, and household chores left little time for amusement, yet the hearty people of Pall Mall made their own fun when they could. There were picnics at the Methodist church, and once in a while a dance in somebody's barn. If it was too cold out there, a family would move their furniture outside and turn the entire house into a dance hall. With a fiddle accompaniment and perhaps an improvised rhythm section of washboard and spoons, neighbors would dance the night away, stopping occasionally to rest and feast on homemade "fixins" the merrymakers brought to share.

Alvin York had sometimes enjoyed these festivities to a fault; those who knew him were wary of his behavior when they thought he might have had too much to drink. Then came the last night of 1914 and a mother's inspired words. Alvin heard her voice with new ears and saw the world through new eyes. Yes, the Lord got ahold of him in that quiet, lamplit cabin as the New Year dawned, and He never let go.

A LITTLE RED POSTCARD

After his New Year's conversion, Alvin was hungry to know more about God and Christ, eager to live life from a new perspective. But where could he turn for information? Though he had the Bible, his mother's example, and a few ministers in the community to talk to, he felt he needed more. Books were scarce in the valley. There were a handful of neighbors who could read well, some like Alvin, who had learned a little and taught himself more, and then those—especially of Mother York's generation—who couldn't write their own names. Alvin wanted to explore the teaching of the Christian faith, and looked forward to the next church revival. Evangelists came to the valley once in a while, but their visits were rare.

Pall Mall seldom saw travelers of any kind. To get in or out of the Wolf River Valley, visitors had to make a tough climb over steep hills. On foot it was hard to travel the twelve miles to

Jamestown and back between sunrise and dark. Few outsiders braved the trek, which made Alvin all the more anxious to welcome the next traveling evangelists to Pall Mall. Wolf River Methodist Church, built in 1840, was the only church in the valley and the largest building for miles around. The simple white frame structure hosted all sorts of meetings and gatherings, public and private. Situated in a creekside nook, the church faced the cemetery across the road where Coonrod Pile and his ancestors were buried.

Early in 1915, Melvin H. Russell came to preach in Pall Mall. He was a "saddlebagger," a circuit-riding minister who traveled from one isolated rural community to the next, holding weeklong revivals. These hearty men went on horseback, their saddlebags stuffed with tracts, Bibles, and their preaching suits. Harsh as the winter weather was, it was a good season for traveling preachers because the days were short, farmwork was light, and people were eager for anything that sparked of novelty or entertainment.

Brother Melvin was a minister of the Church of Christ in Christian Union, a spiritual cousin of the Pentecostal church, headquartered in Circleville, Ohio. His host for the week was Pastor Rosier C. Pile, lay preacher, postmaster, and general store proprietor who was respected as the unofficial leader of the community. York could scarcely wait to learn more about what the Bible taught and how to apply it in his own life. Once the preaching got under way, Brother Melvin impressed Alvin with his "true speaking of the Scriptures." Russell warned his audience in vivid terms about the terrors of punishment in hell and the joys of happiness in heaven for all who followed Christ.

Sunday morning, the last day of the revival, the preacher invited everyone who wanted to give their lives to Jesus to come down front. York stood and moved to the end of the aisle where Brother Melvin waited to shake his hand. He felt like the apostle Paul in the Bible: the things he once loved he now hated. Alvin asked God to forgive him for his years of sinful behavior and self-centeredness. His family, especially Mother York, watched with pride as he walked forward. No doubt others in the congregation nudged each other and nodded in his direction. A wild, cussing, fighting, hard-drinking character like Alvin York making a public profession of faith must have been quite a sight for some of them. *God must be really something if He can change a man like Big 'Un!* They were right: God could change anybody's heart. Alvin would spend the rest of his life as living proof of God's mercy and power.

Alvin called his spiritual transformation "the greatest victory I ever won." The once-notorious brawler added years later, "It's much harder to whip yourself than to whip the other fellow. And I ought to know because I done both."[1] He began faithfully attending the Methodist church, studied the Bible diligently, and came out strongly against drinking. Soon his religious convictions outran what he took to be the Methodist standards. Examining them with newly critical eyes, he detected hypocrisy he hadn't seen before. Folks sitting in the pews seemed to believe one thing six days a week and something else on the seventh. In particular, some of his old moonshining buddies went to church and apparently supported the local congregation's stand against alcohol, while at that very moment their next batch of illegal whiskey was bubbling away somewhere in the woods.

Over the next year, Alvin moved from a point of not paying much attention to what the preacher said in church to believing the church was too lax in upholding the standards of the Bible. By the time Melvin Russell came back to preach again, in December 1915, Alvin had become one of the most faithful and active members of the congregation. Russell and two other pastors came over Bald Mountain from the north on December 29. They had to carry some of their luggage because the trail was so steep the horses couldn't pull their wagon fully loaded. Again Pastor Pile organized the weeklong revival with preaching twice a day. Before the first service, one of Russell's associates, W. W. Loveless, saw a burly, redheaded man walking toward him, "tall and straight as an Indian, dressed in a blue jeans suit and colored shirt." He stuck his hand out and said, "Howdy, preacher." York was there to lead the singing.[2]

Loveless preached that first night from Revelation 12, the story of the angel Michael fighting against the great serpent, Satan, and casting him out of heaven. "Now the devil is down here," Loveless declared, "and we have come to make war on him and his angels in Pall Mall!" The weather was unseasonably warm, and rain pelted the church day after day. The thick, red Tennessee clay stuck to every shoe like wax so that by the end of the night, the church floor was covered with a sheet of it. Every morning men scraped it loose with hoes and shoveled what they could out the door. What was left made such a cloud inside that with all the singing and shouting and stomping, worshippers couldn't see each other across the room. Exhorting, brandishing his Bible, waving his hands in the air, and pacing back and forth across the front of the room, the preacher had to take a short break once in a while to stick his head out the window for a few gulps of fresh air.

At the end of the week, Loveless established a new congregation of the Church of Christ in Christian Union in Pall Mall. The twenty-seven charter members elected Rosier Pile as first elder and Alvin York as second elder. York believed his new denomination and fellow church members would stick more diligently to Bible teaching than the Methodists had. As the three preachers packed up and prepared to leave, the community collected an offering—six dollars in all—to split among them for their service.

Sixty-seven people came to revival that week—practically the whole population of Pall Mall and the surrounding bottomland along the river. One of them was fifteen-year-old Gracie Williams, a shy, blue-eyed blonde who, like Alvin, had been born in the valley and whose family had lived there for generations. The Williams and York farms were close to each other, and Gracie had known Alvin all her life. In fact, Alvin had looked at her in her cradle when he was a boy of twelve and jokingly said, "Someday I'm going to marry that girl."

Until lately, Gracie hadn't been the least interested in Alvin. He was rude and violent, drank too much, fought all the time, and was generally uncomfortable to be around, when he wasn't embarrassing. As little as she cared for him, her father, Asbury Williams, cared even less. No father in his right mind would want his daughter to marry a troublemaker like Alvin York. Over the past year, though, Big 'Un was a changed man. He'd quit drinking and fighting and all the rest. Not only did he come to church, he led the singing. Now he was second elder in a new congregation besides.

Alvin didn't trouble himself with theology or the fine points of Christian conversion. His interest was practical and not theoretical. "My mother's love led me to God," he explained simply. "He showed me the light, and I done followed it." The new Christian Union congregation put up its own white frame building across the river and about half a mile up the road from the Methodist church. Pastor Pile became the preacher, Alvin settled in as official song leader, and both of them taught Sunday school. York took his new duties seriously, walking over the mountain to Byrdstown, Kentucky, once a week for singing lessons.

He also started taking his feelings for Gracie more seriously. He'd wanted to court her earlier but had somehow sensed he was too coarse and wild to attract any girl. Now he thought he had a chance, but Asbury Williams thought otherwise. He was dead set against Alvin and Gracie spending time together. In a place so small and tight-knit as Pall Mall, there was nowhere the two of them could talk without everybody finding out, and Alvin didn't want to make life awkward for Gracie by defying her father.

One day either Alvin or Gracie made a happy discovery. Gracie used a footpath running between the York and Williams farms to bring the cows in at dusk. This path was also a handy route to the woods where Alvin liked to hunt rabbits, squirrels, and wild turkeys. Alvin later admitted that he "most awful sudden found out there were a heap of squirrels along that old lane."[3] More important, there was a spot by the riverbank where the path dipped down enough behind a rise so that anyone standing there couldn't be seen at a distance. Once the two discovered this lucky accident of topography, they met there almost every day. It was the spot where, in time, Alvin asked Gracie to marry him. She didn't want to disobey her father and wasn't sure what to do. She loved Alvin, yet wanted to make sure marriage was the right step. As they spoke that afternoon, Gracie's shyness kept her voice low; sometimes it quivered because she was so nervous. She couldn't yet say yes, but hoped the day would come when she could. So they met and parted day after day at sunset, with Gracie walking home across the field, calling her cows. Alvin sat on a favorite log, his hunting dogs sprawled at his feet, and watched her until she got to the Williams house and went inside.

In the spring of 1916 the *Fentress County Gazette* reported that a highway was coming through town. Federal Aid Road 28, also called the Dixie Short Route, would run across Tennessee on its way from the Gulf Coast to St. Louis, ending Pall Mall's long isolation. There were also two railroads planning extensions into the county, which meant residents no longer had to go fifty miles by horse and wagon to Oneida to catch the nearest train.

These projects promised steady work for local men, and Alvin planned to add road building to his list of jobs. He was already farming his mother's seventy-five acres with his brothers' help, blacksmithing, and working on Pastor Pile's farm for a dollar a day plus board. Soon he joined the Dixie Short Route crew, earning $1.60 for a ten-hour day spent cutting trees, breaking rocks, and hauling gravel. He still found time to hunt with his coon dogs almost every night, and to compete in the shooting matches he enjoyed and excelled in. It was a good life. To top it all off, now he was in love with the most wonderful girl in the world, and the two of them had agreed to marry if Mr. Williams would give his consent. He could imagine building a house for his bride on his mother's land and spending the rest of his life happily raising a family on the banks of the Wolf, like so many generations before him had done.

That future disappeared in an instant on June 5, 1917, with the arrival of a little red postcard from Washington, D.C. It was from the federal government, ordering Alvin York to register with the local draft board. Every man between eighteen and forty-five years old in the county got a card just like it. On April 6 the United States had declared war on Germany, which had been fighting against much of Europe since the summer of 1914 and threatened America's allies Britain and France. Alvin and his friends could have read about the war in the local newspaper or in the occasional paper a visitor might bring from Nashville. But the thought that a war four thousand miles away might affect their lives likely never occurred to them. Now the country was mobilizing for war and drafting able-bodied men into military service.

Alvin was a brave man, and a strong one. He was probably a better marksman than the best sharpshooter the army had. He would make an excellent soldier. Except that he didn't believe it was God's will for one man to kill another. The sixth commandment was unequivocal in Alvin's mind: "Thou shalt not kill" (Ex. 20:13). As part of his religious conversion, York had become a pacifist. The onetime knife-wielding brawler now believed men and women were made in the image of God and that one man had no right to take another man's life. If a man was evil or wrong, Alvin trusted in God to sort matters out in His own time. He knew he could not kill another human being.

At the same time, Alvin was a true patriot who took pride in American freedom. He now respected the law and followed it responsibly. His was an impossible situation: a law-abiding citizen called by his country to defy God's commandment.

He turned to Pastor Pile for advice. On top of his other duties, Pile was a member of the Fentress County draft board. He could see the impasse from both sides, as a preacher and as a draft board official. "I've been converted to the gospel of peace and love and of 'Do good for evil,'" Alvin reminded Pastor

Pile. He'd once been a fighter, but he had never killed anybody and didn't want to start now. "I turned my back on all those rowdy things and found a heap of comfort and happiness in religion . . . I believe in the Bible, and the Bible says, 'Thou shalt not kill.' That's so definite a child can understand it."[4]

Once that postcard came from Washington, Alvin and his pastor talked day after day about what to do. Alvin spent long stretches alone with his dogs on the wooded hillsides around the valley, reading his Bible and praying for direction. He'd take that red card out of his pocket and read it again, turning it over with his thick fingers and puzzling about what to do. There was no doubt he had to register, but it was possible to be excused from duty on religious grounds as a conscientious objector, someone whose faith led him to believe all fighting was wrong.

Pastor Pile helped him write a letter to the draft board, requesting exemption as "a member of a well-recognized sect or organization" whose beliefs "forbade its members to participate in war in any form." Within days the board wrote back, denying his request because, they said, "We do not think 'The Church of Christ in Christian Union' is a well-recognized religious sect," and because that church's only creed was the Bible, which was subject to individual interpretation on the question of participating in a war. Pile helped Alvin write a letter of appeal to the district board in Nashville, with both of them adding notarized statements of their belief that all war was wrong. The appeal was denied.

Fentress County's first draft quota was called up on September 23, so Alvin knew it would only be a matter of time before his time came. He was ordered to Jamestown for a physical, and made the trip on foot, passing places along the Dixie Short Route right-of-way he was helping to clear. Alvin was in excellent health, twenty-nine years old, six feet even, and 170 pounds of rock-breaking, blacksmithing muscle. He passed.

Back home he gave Pastor Pile the news and then went to tell his mother, who cried (for only the second time Alvin ever remembered) at the thought that her boy would be sent into harm's way so far off. She'd traveled very little in her life; France was unimaginable to her, though she had faith that God would keep her son safe. Alvin also shared the sad truth with his dear Gracie. They'd have to postpone getting married, but promised to stay true to each other and marry when Alvin came home.

Alvin kept his job on the road crew until November 10, when Pastor Pile himself brought a blue postcard out to him in the middle of the day while he was driving steel. The card directed Alvin C. York to be ready for military service on twenty-four hours' notice. Four days later he was ordered to report for duty in the U.S. armed forces. He thought about running away to the mountains. He thought about staying in Pall Mall to see what would happen. But in the end, he said goodbye to beautiful Gracie, his family, and friends; packed a small suitcase; and walked the twelve miles to Jamestown.

Alvin and the twenty others called up along with him spent

the night in town, then traveled to the train station in Oneida, eagerly taking in the sights of new places, the paved highway that seemed to go on forever, and all those automobiles on the road. They'd left Jamestown early in the morning, then, in typical "hurry up and wait" military fashion, sat around the depot until after midnight. York was farther from home than he'd ever been and was already miserably homesick. Finally, at 2:00 a.m. the line of southbound coaches came chuffing in. Alvin watched wide-eyed; he'd never seen a train before. He stepped aboard and headed for Camp Gordon, near Augusta, where within another day he was no longer Alvin C. York, but Private York, serial number 1910421, United States Army.

THOU SHALT NOT KILL

The day he got his draft notice, York started keeping a journal, jotting down occasional thoughts with a pencil in a small notebook he could slip into his shirt pocket. He wasn't much of a writer, and the only two books he'd read in his life were the Bible and a biography of Jesse James. Yet he sensed that his little red postcard was the beginning of an adventure worth remembering. On the flyleaf of his notebook he wrote, "A history of the places where I have bin." His story began, "Pall Mall, Tennessee. Well, the first notice I received was to go and register. So I did." At Camp Gordon he recorded his first official military duty—picking up cigarette butts. "I thought that was pretty hard as I didn't smoke, but I did it just the same." Away from the Tennessee hills for the first time, he thought the flat, sandy Georgia landscape was dreary. "There ain't no strength or seasoning in it," he wrote. "It shore needs hills and mountains most awful bad."[1]

After two months of basic training, York was assigned in February 1918 to Company G, 328th Battalion, 82nd Division, known as the "All-American" Division from its proud claim to have soldiers from every state. Twenty percent of the men in the 82nd were foreign-born, and York's 1st Platoon of Company G had the biggest variety of all. The Tennessean had never seen a foreigner before, so these men fascinated him with their heavy accents, strange ways, and tough behavior. To Private York they were "the toughest and most hard-boiled doughboys [slang for American soldiers] I ever heard tell of. There were bartenders, saloon bouncers, ice men, coal miners, dirt farmers, actors, mill hands, and city boys who had growed up in the back alleys and learned to scrap ever since they were knee high to a duck. They could out-swear, out-drink, and out-cuss any other crowd of men I have ever knowed." Some of them teased Alvin about being so passive and innocent, but couldn't get a rise out of him. "I didn't want to fight nobody," he wrote in his diary, "and least of all American doughboys."

His army-issue rifle was far easier to handle than the heavy old muzzle loaders, called "hog rifles," he'd used all his life in the mountains. But in many instances, especially at close range, the muzzle loader was more accurate. He surely took much better care of his guns than whoever had had his last. That "old gun was just full of Greece" at first, but with some time and attention, he got it cleaned up to suit him. Alvin couldn't remember when he didn't know how to shoot. He chuckled quietly on the firing range, watching "them there Greeks and Italians and

Poles and New York Jews" completely miss not only the targets but the dirt backstop behind them as well. It was no trouble for York to score one bull's-eye after another on "them great big army targets. They were so much bigger than turkey's heads." One of the shooting competitions he had mastered back home was hitting a turkey tethered behind a log when the bird bobbed its head up.

One day, when the company lined up in formation, the company commander, Captain E. C. B. Danforth, asked the men if any of them kept a journal. There was a regulation against it, for fear that they might be captured and that the enemy could get useful information from what they'd written.

"I'm not saying whether I do or don't, sir," York answered.

"A diary will betray you and your comrades if you're ever captured," Danforth warned.

"Sir, I didn't come to the war to be captured. I'm not going to be captured. If the Germans ever get any information out of me, they'll have to get it out of my dead body."

Neither of them said any more, and Private York kept his diary.

Captain Danforth thought there was something special about York. He was so plainspoken, so honest, so eager to do what was right, that the captain pegged him for a natural leader. Danforth was a Georgian, Harvard Class of 1915, years younger and far more sophisticated than the Tennessee mountaineer, but the two developed a strong personal respect for each other. It was only natural that York would go to Danforth for advice when the matter of his conscientious objector status came up again.

After the draft board in Nashville denied his appeal, York hadn't pursued the issue. But Mother York and Pastor Pile kept working to get Alvin a deferment. Pile appealed to the War Department for a religious exemption, and he also helped Mother York submit a claim that she was a widow and Alvin was her sole support. These two requests worked their way through the Washington bureaucracy and down to Camp Gordon. Finally the Department ruled that York could be exempted on religious grounds. If he would sign and return the forms they gave him, he would be certified a conscientious objector and excused from service.

However, when faced with the decision, York couldn't sign the exemption form with a clear conscience. He believed the Bible taught that war was wrong, but he also believed a Christian should serve his country. He prayed for an answer and read his Bible faithfully, searching for what God would have him do. Weeks went by, and still he was stymied. Company G would be deployed overseas soon. If he was going to get out of the army, he had to make his choice.

Sometime in March 1918, Private York went to Captain Danforth with the whole story. He explained that he wanted to serve his country and do his part, but that the Bible was clear that a Christian couldn't kill. "I'll keep being a soldier if I have to," he said. "I'll go overseas. I'll even kill Germans if you order me to. But I don't believe in killing nohow, and it worries me plenty."[2]

Danforth discussed York's struggle with his battalion commander, Colonel George Edward Buxton. The colonel was a wise and patient man, well equipped to lead such an ethnic potpourri as the 328th. A Rhode Island native with a high social pedigree, Danforth was a former war correspondent and a personal friend of Theodore Roosevelt. He and Captain Danforth both saw York's sincerity and his genuine concern for doing what was right. Buxton suggested to Danforth that the two of them talk to York together.

A few nights later, York was ordered by his captain to report with him to Major Buxton's quarters. Before leaving his barracks, York knelt in prayer, asking God to guide him. Then he picked up his Bible and joined the captain.

The major welcomed them to his Spartan quarters furnished with a bed, a few camp stools, and a trunk in the corner. A single lightbulb hung from a cord in the middle of the ceiling. Buxton opened by saying he didn't bring them in to address them as their battalion commander, but for them to exchange ideas as "three American citizens interested in a common cause. I respect any honest religious conviction," he added, "and am here to talk through them man to man."

The major asked York why he didn't want to fight. York said it was because he belonged to a church "that disbelieves in fighting and killing." He explained that the church's only creed was the Bible, and the Bible was against killing.

"What do you find in the Bible that's against war?" the major asked.

"The Bible says, 'Thou shalt not kill,'" York answered.

"Do you accept everything in the Bible—every sentence, every word—as completely as you accept the sixth commandment?"

"Yes, sir, I do."

Buxton picked up his own Bible and turned to Luke 22. "He that hath no sword, let him sell his garment, and buy one," he read aloud (v. 36). "Is that in the Bible?"

York said that it was, then countered with a verse of his own. "Whosoever shall smite thee on thy right cheek, turn to him the other also" (Matt. 5:39).

"Yes, the Bible says that," the colonel agreed. But, he asked, "Do you believe that the Christ who drove the money changers from the temple with a whip would stand up and do nothing when the helpless Belgian people were overrun and driven from their homes?"

York thought this was a serious question. The private and the major, with Captain Danforth joining in sometimes, talked and read aloud from the Bible for more than an hour. York pointed out that the Bible taught that whoever lived by the sword would die by the sword, and that Christ preached, "Blessed are the meek: for they shall inherit the earth" (Matt. 5:5). Buxton countered with Jesus' instruction, "Render . . . unto Caesar the things which are Caesar's" (Matt. 22:21). Christians, he said, had a responsibility to fight when their liberties were at stake. Buxton ended their conversation with a passage from Ezekiel 33, where the prophet warns the city watchmen to be diligent and blow the warning trumpet in case of enemy attack:

Then whosoever heareth the sound of the trumpet, and taketh not warning; if the sword come, and take him away, his blood shall be upon his own head . . . But if the watchman see the sword come, and blow not the trumpet, and the people be not warned; if the sword come, and take any person from among them, he is taken away in his iniquity; but his blood will I require at the watchman's hand. (vv. 4, 6)

Was York the watchman? Was God calling him to stand up for innocent Belgians and French women and children being murdered in their homes? He sat there in the dim light of the single bulb, more confused than ever. Looking into the major's eyes, he realized they reminded him of his father's.

"I'd like some time to think it over, Major," he said finally. He promised that in the meantime he'd "go on just as I have been, doing everything I'm told to do and trying to be a good soldier." Major Buxton told him to take all the time he needed. Later that night, lying sleepless in his bunk, Private York reached for his journal, its red cloth cover already stained and worn from use.

Camp Gordon, Georgia. Oh, these were trying hours for a boy like me, trying to live for God and do His blessed will, but yet I could look up and say:

O Master, let me walk with Thee
In lonely paths of service free,

Tell me Thy secret, help me to bear
The strain of toil, the fret of care.

And then the Lord would bless me and help me to bear my hard toils.

Time passed, and York tried to think hard about whether or not to go to war. But in the army camp he couldn't find the solitude to focus his thoughts. The captain granted him a ten-day leave to go home and think it over. On March 19 he took the train back to Oneida and happened to see a Jamestown resident who drove him to Fentress County in his car. York walked the last twelve miles to Pall Mall, carrying his suitcase. He went to Pastor Pile right away, and for days on end the two talked about the question. Mother York prayed for him, and Gracie did too.

As the ten days ticked away, Alvin grew still more frustrated. Nothing seemed to bring him any closer to an answer. Then he thought of his favorite spot high on a hillside, where he could see the whole valley stretched out below, and the only sounds were the river and the wind. He'd gone there before when he had to think hard about something. It was where he'd sorted out his thoughts about religion after his life-changing New Year's experience, and where he'd sat as he decided whether to ask Gracie to marry him. It was a long climb up to a spot at the base of two huge rocks that sat side by side, visible from the valley floor. Some people called them the Yellow Doors, and some called them Bible Rock because they looked kind of like an open Bible. With only his dogs for company, he made the long journey up, built a fire, and opened his Bible.

He read and prayed and talked to himself hour after hour. Midnight came and went, and still Alvin never felt tired. He begged God to show him the way. Almost before he knew it, the sky began to lighten, the birds started to sing, and curls of smoke from cabins that dotted the valley floor signaled that wives and daughters were starting breakfast. Later, he wrote:

As I prayed there alone, a great peace kind of come into my soul and a great calm come over me, and I received my assurance. [God] heard my prayer and He come to me on the mountainside. I didn't see Him, of course, but he was there just the same. I knowed he was there. He understood that I didn't want to be a fighter or a killing man, that I didn't want to go to war to hurt nobody nohow. And yet I wanted to do what my country wanted me to do. I wanted to serve God and my country, too. He understood all of this. He seen right inside of me, and He knowed I had been troubled and worried, not because I was afraid, but because I put Him first, even before my country, and I only wanted to do what would please Him.

So He took pity on me and He gave me the assurance I needed. I didn't understand everything. I didn't understand how He could let me go to war and even kill and yet not hold that against me. I didn't even want to understand. It was His will and that was enough for me. So at last I begun to see the light. I begun to understand that no matter what a man is forced to do, so long as he is right in his own soul he remains a righteous man. I knowed I would go to war. I knowed I would be protected from all harm, and that so long as I believed in Him He would not allow even a hair of my head to be harmed.[3]

It was settled: Alvin York, Christian, would go to war. As the morning sun rose over the valley rim, York headed for his cabin, singing as he went.

O God, in hope that sends the shining ray,
Far down the future's broadening way,
In peace that only Thou canst give,
With Thee, O Master, let me live.

He said good-bye to his mother and spent a tender moment with Gracie under a big beech tree on the path where they had met so many times before.

"I'll come back for you," he told her confidently.

"God be with you, Alvin," she said, her eyes welling with tears.

Back at Camp Gordon he started second-guessing himself. Was he doing the right thing? He listened to his barracks mates talk about the fighting ahead of them. How had they balanced their personal beliefs with a call to arms? They didn't seem to think about it at all. On top of his indecision, he got an envelope from the Office of the President of the United States. Pastor

Pile had written directly to President Wilson, asking for a religious exemption for Private York. Someone in the president's office had forwarded the pastor's letter for York's comment. York never responded.

Company G left Camp Gordon for Camp Upton, New York, on April 19, 1918. On the twenty-third Alvin wrote his last letter to Gracie before sailing overseas. As always, he shaped the words carefully, laboring to keep his lines straight on the page. He didn't know how long it would be before he could write her again. In fact, there was a chance this would be his last letter. Alvin filled page after page, pouring his heart out to the girl he loved so much, trusting their future to the will of God. "I want to hear from you once more before I sail, ho ho," he wrote. "For I love you." He continued:

> I mean by the Grace of God to come back to you some day. And say darling, I am so glad to know that you have promised to be True to me until I come back. I sure will be true to you darling, and if I should never get back to you darling, you can say that your best Lover and your Truest Sweetheart is gone. But please remember if you meet me there you will have to git right with God.
>
> I am longing to see you. But I will sail for france in a bout ten days I guess at the longest, and I sure want to hear from you before I go. For its you I love. Oh yes Gracie there is not a day nor a night but what you are on my mind. Oh I never had so great love for no one as I have for you . . .

If I get killed you can say that I died that you might stay free . . . And listen darling if I don't never git back will you go and stay with Mother? That is my request, for Mother will have plenty of money [his $10,000 government life insurance] and she sure will take care of you . . . Oh say darling I can't never be satisfied as long are you are talking to the other boys so please promise me that you will not go with one while I am in France . . . [When I left you in November] you remember you were crying and I asked you not to let eney other boys kiss you and asked you to promise me that and you said you would not let eney one kiss you. So I hope you will hold your promise and be true.

. . . I am coming back if the Lord permits and I hope he will . . . So don't think I will forget you. So good-bye from your loving sweetheart, with a kiss.

Alvin C. York[4]

Company G traveled to Boston on April 30, where they would board transports for France. That day Captain Danforth lined his men up and asked each of them individually if they were willing to sail overseas to fight. When he came to York, the private answered that he didn't object to fighting. "The only thing that bothers me is, are we in the right or in the wrong?"

After a short conversation, the captain concluded, "Blessed are the peacemakers."

"If a man can make peace by fighting, he is a peacemaker," York replied.

"And so, do you object to fighting the Germans?"

"No, sir, I do not."

Before dawn on May 1, York and the rest of the battalion boarded a Scandinavian ship for the sixteen-day voyage to Liverpool. York had never seen the ocean before and was awed by the sight of it. Unfortunately, the first promising impression was overwhelmed by a miserable bout of seasickness. He noticed that other soldiers seemed to take the rolling seas in stride. "The Greeks, Italians, Poles, and New York Jews stood the trip right smart," he wrote in his diary. "It sort of made up for their bad shooting."

York spent five days in England, where he looked in amazement at the lush gardens and tidy houses, declaring they must have special gardeners every few acres to keep everything looking so perfect. Crossing the English Channel from Southampton to Le Havre took only a few hours, but to Private York it seemed like forever. "Long before we landed I didn't care whether we stayed up or went down, whether we got there or didn't get there," he wrote, adding that the ride felt like a bucking mule. "I didn't care about anything."

Company G was issued new equipment, including new rifles. These were Eddystone Enfields, made by Remington in Eddystone, Pennsylvania, based on the 1917 British Enfield design but modified to accept American ammunition. The soldiers were also issued gas masks, a reminder that frontline battle would be coming soon. They each received two new pairs of boots, the idea being that one pair could dry while the other was being worn. To avoid hauling the extra weight, most soldiers quickly discarded the spares.

The first leg of York's trip from the coast to the battlefront was in a boxcar labeled "40 men or 8 horses." Walking by, he heard an enlisted man say, "Captain, I loaded the forty men all right, but if you put the eight horses in too, they'll trample the boys to death." In Floraville the battalion was inspected by General John J. "Blackjack" Pershing. Though York was a head taller than the commanding general, he thought Pershing looked every inch the leader and believed the general was impressed with how well the 328th marched. One onlooker observed that with his ramrod-straight posture and uniforms custom-made on London's Savile Row, Pershing was "tailor-made for monuments." York chuckled to think what Pershing's reaction would have been if he'd seen the battalion a few months ago when they were clumsy new recruits. They had come a long way since then.

Once in a while the men got permission to go into a local town for an evening's entertainment, but York never went along. He'd had all the drinking and fighting he ever wanted in his life, and so he stayed behind, reading his Bible and writing in his notebook. A day of bayonet practice stirred up feelings about his commitment to fight. Could he stab a flesh-and-blood human being, even a German, at close range, like he stabbed those practice dummies? Was he justified in killing a man to keep him from killing somebody else? He mused, "Though I knowed we were fighting for peace, still it made me feel queer to think I might have to cut up human beings."

On the night of June 26, Company G marched out of the village of Rambucourt to man the trenches for the first time. Artillery rumbled in the distance, and as they marched they passed fresh graves topped with rough crosses. Occasionally, a rifle bullet would whistle through the marching formation, but the men were far enough from the lines that the bullets were too spent to be dangerous. As the ranks continued forward, the bullets came with more power, and some of the men started ducking.

"It's no use ducking," one of them called out to nobody in particular. "You never hear the one that gets you."

"GOD HELPED ME OUT"

During the summer of 1918, the 328th held Company G in reserve, assigning them to relatively quiet sections of the line, then rotating them to safe positions in the rear. The men were spoiling for a fight. York wrote that they were ready "to go out on top of the trenches and start something. Those Greeks and Italians and the New York Jews, ho ho, they didn't want to lie around and do nothing. They were always ready to go over the top, almost too anxious." The inexperienced soldiers wanted to run out and get the job done, but without planning and proper flanking support, they were sure to be picked off by German sharpshooters.

The Great War in France had stalled at a line of trenches running more than three hundred miles across the country. The Germans had originally anchored their offensive line at Alsace in the east, then planned to sweep down from Belgium like a giant hinge, driving the French ahead of them. But the offensive had stalled, the two sides had dug in, and there they stayed month after month, shelling and being shelled. The Americans had joined the war to give the French and their English allies enough manpower to push the hinge back open and drive the Germans northward out of France. While leaders gathered their forces and made their plans, there was little for the new American arrivals to do.

Living conditions in the trenches were miserable almost beyond description. One machine gunner did his best: "Lice, rats, barbed wire, fleas, shells, bombs, underground caves, corpses, blood, liquor, mice, cats, artillery, filth, bullets, mortar, fire, steel: That is what war is." Years of shelling had churned the ground into a gelatinous quagmire that never dried. Even in so hellish a place, Private York was sure the Lord would take care of him. "There is no use of worrying a bout Shells," he wrote in his diary, "for you cant keep them from busting in your trench nor you cant Stop the rain . . . So what is the use of worrying if you can't alter things just ask God to help you and accept them and make the best of them by the help of God; yet some men do worry, and By Doing So they effectually destroy their peace of Mind without doing any one any good."

On July 8 York was promoted to private first class. By then he was in charge of a squad armed with French automatic rifles called Chauchats, which the Americans pronounced "show-shows." These were heavy, inaccurate, tripod-mounted weapons that none of the soldiers liked, but which York and his men carried on patrols. They never met a single German during these sorties, though they took occasional sniper fire. The humming sound bullets made as they passed reminded York of bumblebees back home when he robbed their nest. Taking his turn in the trenches, York heard shells exploding and bullets "a-singing a round my head. Yet," he assured Gracie, "I stayed there Day and Night and I just trusted the Lord and I never got hurt. So if you will always trust the Lord he will always take you through safe."[1]

On July 20 York told Gracie he'd received his first letter from her in France, which had taken thirty days to travel from Pastor Pile's post office in Pall Mall to the trenches near the town of Rambucourt. He could only write a little, he explained, because he couldn't get any more paper, and he wanted to save some for a letter to his mother. Also, he reported, "I had to quit writing you for a few minutes. Just now the Germans was sending some shells over there was 15 shells struck within a few yards of me but I never got hurt."[2]

Company G marched into a picturesque village called Pont-à-Mousson on the Moselle River, seemingly untouched by four years of shelling. Evidently some informal local agreement had spared the place, and in the middle of a devastated area, it was an oasis of order, cleanliness, plentiful food, and friendly locals. York wrote to his sweetheart that "those French girls stood there talking and I couldnt understand a word they said. I didnt understand what they wanted until they showed me, ho ho." York and his unit spent a week on the front at Liverdun beginning August 24, and when they returned, Pont-à-Mousson was completely deserted, with tables set for lunch and food still cooking on the stoves. Warned that they were about to be shelled at last, the villagers had escaped with only whatever they could carry. American soldiers gladly helped themselves to the homemade dishes simmering on the fire. Germans began their attack, and the Americans moved to a safe area on the riverbank to camp. Artillery blasts destroyed the beautiful vineyards and orchards around the town. Allied shells fired from battleships on the coast screamed overhead on their way to targets fifteen miles farther inland. As soldiers watched in wonder, airplanes buzzed and clattered overhead, then engaged the German flyers in circling, swooping dogfights.

After a few more days beside the Moselle, the 328th Infantry Battalion headed for the town of St. Mihiel and their first taste of active frontline combat. This medieval town was at the southern tip of a salient, an isolated forward thrust the Germans had made into French-held territory during the first months of the war and held ever since. The area was rich in iron ore, and the invaders mined it to supply their arms manufacturers with weapons-grade steel. Faced with the huge numbers of American reinforcements pouring in, the kaiser realized he could never hold all his forward positions, and this was one he'd decided to abandon. American generals hoped to press the enemy as they withdrew, then push on past the trenches into occupied northern and eastern France. The Germans started their movement on September 11. The next morning, American guns opened up on the retreating enemy, and the 328th advanced against the invaders they called "the Bosch."

Alvin had been promoted a second time, and Corporal York was now a squad leader. He continued to marvel at his men's reckless enthusiasm in wanting always to get ahead of the line of advance, and also at what bad shots they were. They seemed to shoot a lot more at the ground and the sky than at whatever might be in front of them. The Bosch retreated eastward, firing poison gas as they went. At dusk the Americans camped in the town of Norroy, where a beautiful vineyard attracted a group of hungry and thirsty soldiers who thought they were safe from attack. But an observation balloon spotted them and directed artillery fire at the vineyard, wounding several of the men. As a result, American officers placed the vineyard off-limits.

Usually York thought about Gracie at night, but this time all he could think about was those tempting grapes up the road. At last he decided to pay the vineyard a visit, walking off to the side of the road in the dark to avoid the American sentries. Suddenly a shell exploded and York went running, colliding with another soldier in the shadows off the roadbed. Before York could figure out whether this was the moment when he would kill or be killed in hand-to-hand combat, a flash of artillery revealed the face of Captain Danforth.

"Corporal York," the captain barked, "there are orders forbidding troops in this area!"

"Yes, sir."

"I would say also, Corporal, that these grapes taste mighty good."

"Yes, sir."

After only two days of fighting, the Allies chased the Bosch out of the St. Mihiel salient, and by September 16 the area was secure. It was the first time York had been on the offensive, and the first time he saw anybody killed by enemy fire. Recalling those days, he said, "There is no tongue or human being who can ever tell the feeling of a man during this time. But I never doubted in the thickest of the battle but what God would bring me through safe."

The Americans were reopening the hinge of the German battle line, swinging the western end of the front so as to make the line of battle run more north-south, forcing the Germans back across their prewar border with France. This meant a heavy concentration of offensive units to the north and west. Allied leaders planned to throw everything they had—160 divisions—at the enemy, but would stagger them at different times so the Germans wouldn't know where the next strike would come. Six hundred thousand Americans and 225,000 French soldiers would stage a massive, all-out offensive in the Meuse-Argonne sector to defeat Germany before winter weather set in.

The 328th rested in St. Mihiel for a week, then headed for their assigned spot in the big push, sixty-five miles northwest at Mézières and Sedan, where there was an important railroad junction. To get there they had to cross the Meuse River and march through the dense Argonne Forest, supposedly bristling with German defenders. The Argonne was a superb place for defensive action because the trees were so thick, and because high, tangled undergrowth made the terrain difficult to march through and provided plentiful cover for snipers.

Before the final long march on foot, the men traveled part of the way in boxcars, then in buses driven by French colonials from Indochina, who evidently had never driven buses or anything else. York wrote that he'd "done never seen a Chinaman before" and that they "must have sort of had the idea they had to get us there before they even started" and drove like maniacs. Two buses flipped before the trip was over, but nobody was seriously hurt. As the weather turned cold and rainy, the 328th mustered with the rest of the 82nd American Division and prepared to chase the Bosch out of France for good.

At 5:30 on the morning of September 26, 1918, the first Allied forces marched into the Argonne Forest to begin what General Pershing planned as the final offensive of the war. Retreating Germans gave ground easily until the Americans were in the thick of the forest. Beginning about two miles in, the high underbrush was booby-trapped with coils of barbed wire, and hidden machine guns seemed to spit deadly fire from every direction. The offensive stalled in the middle of the forest on October 1. After a few days of rest and resupply, fresh troops came up, including the 328th. On October 5, Corporal Alvin York marched into the forest to root out the enemy.

The closer York got to the action, the busier the road was. The way would have been crowded enough in good weather, but rain drizzled down incessantly, turning the surface into knee-deep muck made deeper by supply trucks, mule-drawn wagons, and hundreds of thousands of infantry boots. As motorized vehicles broke down and gun caissons slid into ditches, swearing soldiers slogged wearily around them. When horses dropped dead from exhaustion, soldiers left them where they fell, unbuckled the harnesses, and pulled the wagons themselves.

A week earlier the French premier, Georges Clemenceau, was determined to have a look at the front as the final great offensive got under way. General Pershing explained that the roads were bad and choked with traffic, and that only essential vehicles would be allowed. Determined to be where the action was, Clemenceau set off for the Argonne in his enormous car. The closer he got to the front, the slower traffic moved, until he was completely boxed in. Soldiers streaming around him muttered about "just another damn politician blocking a lifeline with a black limousine." Furthermore, the road was so narrow and muddy that there was no room to back up or maneuver. Defeated at last, the premier rolled down the window and ordered a squad of men to pick up his car and turn it around. The soldiers dropped their packs; lifted the slippery, mud-covered car out of the ooze; and set it down, headed in the other direction.

York marched on, seeing wounded men passing him on their way to the rear. A machine gun nest hidden in the brush opened fire on the other side of the road, mowing down members of his company while Alvin watched in horror. To stop and fight enemies they couldn't see would only make them more of a target, so they hurried faster toward the gunfire. York spoke to himself in a low voice:

O Jesus, the great rock of foundation
Whereon my feet were set with sovereign grace
Through shells or death with all their agitation,
Thou wilt protect me if I will only trust in Thy grace.
Bless Thy Holy Name.

The trees thinned out as the troops advanced, splintered and uprooted by relentless artillery fire, and the stream of wounded became a flood. Men hit by artillery lay beside the road moaning in pain or dead, their eyes and mouths frozen open in expressions of horror.

Reaching the northern part of the Argonne Forest, the 82nd Division fell in behind the 1st Division as the 1st fought for what the field maps called Hill 223. Here, near the edge of the forest, was a hill the Germans wanted to hold on to. At the foot of its western slope was a narrow-gauge railroad that brought supplies to the front and carried wounded men and iron ore out. The Americans' immediate objective was to go over the hill and down the other side, capturing the rail line. The time of attack, H-Hour, was set for 6:00 a.m., October 8, 1918. It was the day Alvin C. York of Pall Mall, Tennessee, would become one of the most famous soldiers in American history.[3]

The attack was supposed to begin with an artillery barrage, but the time came and went without a shot being fired. Gunners had trouble getting their field pieces in position because of the mud. It was tricky forming up offensive ranks in the dark and in the high brush. Even as the horizon began to lighten, soldiers could scarcely see through the mist and fog. At ten minutes past six, the signal came to advance without artillery. Company G was on the left section of the 328th battle line and headed over the top of the hill with other units. It was only two kilometers (about a mile and a quarter) from the crest down the slope to the railroad, but the Germans would make them pay for every step. As soon as the Allied helmets appeared, enemy machine gun emplacements at the bottom of the hill and on the hillside across the valley opened up with deadly effect. Men were cut down in waves that reminded Corporal York of a mowing machine going through a hayfield.

Battalions to the right and left were pinned down, which left the still-advancing 328th isolated and unprotected ahead of the rest of the line. Company G was in the worst position of all, at the left flank of the forward line and suddenly exposed to fire from three sides. The 1st Division, which had gone in before the 328th, was stalled in a salient ahead of them. The Germans began a pincer movement to cut off and surround the 1st, with Company G directly in the path of the pincer jaws at the salient base.

Captain Danforth could see that as long as the German machine gunners kept firing from the opposite hillside, the Allies on his line were helpless. They would either be butchered trying to advance through a hail of Spandau fire or be killed or captured in the pincer movement. He ordered the platoon sergeant from 1st Platoon to send out a patrol to see if they could do anything about those machine gun emplacements.

The patrol was commanded by Corporal Bernard Early and included squads led by Corporals William C. Cutting, Murray Savage, and Alvin C. York. At 6:00 a.m. the three squads had totaled twenty-four men; by now there were seventeen soldiers left.

Early led his men single file away from the line of fire, past the left flank and into enemy territory. After a few minutes they stopped to consider whether they should attack the enemy from that point or keep circling around and hit them from behind. They decided to keep moving, following a natural ravine that had been widened to form a shallow trench.

With no warning, two German stretcher bearers appeared out of the high brush and mist. Seeing the Americans, they dropped their empty stretcher and ran. When the Americans ordered them to stop, one obeyed, but the other kept running and disappeared. The patrol took off after him, hoping to catch him before he could give them away. They'd only gone a short distance in pursuit before literally stumbling upon twenty or thirty members of a Prussian reserve division having their breakfast. The reservists had put their weapons aside to eat, and only one officer was armed. After a few shots, the Prussians surrendered, but as the Americans formed their POWs into a line, the officer shouted to the machine gunners, who opened fire. Within seconds, the deadly Spandaus had killed six Americans and wounded three, while leaving their own countrymen uninjured. Corporal Cutting was hit three times, Corporal Early six times, and Corporal Savage, York's bunkmate, was killed by so many rounds his uniform was almost torn off. Every other soldier in Savage's squad was dead; York's squad had one dead and one with a bullet in his shoulder.

That left seven privates and Corporal York to carry out their mission. As the ranking soldier, York took command of the remnants of his patrol and about two dozen prisoners.

When the machine guns resumed firing, the Germans and the Americans still alive flattened themselves on the ground, except for Corporal York. As he watched the gunners, he noticed they raised their heads up before they fired in order not to hit their own men lying in the grass. The sight reminded him of turkey shoots back home, where contestants shot at a turkey's head when it popped up from behind a log. Describing the scene later, he explained, "In order to sight me or swing their machine guns at me, the Germans had to show their heads above the trenches [actually the gun emplacements] and every time I saw a head I just teched it off." Corporal York yelled at the gunners to stop firing and surrender, but they kept shooting, and he realized it was either him or them. Whenever a head popped up, York "teched it off" without a miss, since, as he noted, Germans' heads were a lot bigger than turkeys'. Firing from a prone position in the grass, York silenced one machine gun nest after another.

As the gunners fell, the shooting became less intense. Once the protective brush around York was shot up, he thought he might as well aim from a better position and stood, firing offhand. When he ran out of rifle ammunition, he switched to his

own Colt .45 that he always carried. A German lieutenant led a
bayonet charge against York with six men. York saw them coming and quickly thought of another Pall Mall shooting lesson.
Hunting ducks, York had learned that if he shot the lead bird in a
formation first, the others would scatter. But if he shot the birds
back to front, the others would keep flying and give him clean
targets. Even though the first bayonet was already dangerously
close, York fired at the last man in line first. The corporal had
six shots for six attackers, so that one miss would be deadly. But
he didn't miss, dropping them all in rapid succession, the first
one last and nearly within a bayonet length. Turning around, he
saw that in all the confusion the German officer he'd captured
still had his pistol. York ordered him to hand it over and felt that
it was hot: the German had been shooting at York's back while
he was facing the bayonet attack.

Enemy fire continued to taper off, and the corporal's next
responsibility was to determine how to get his men and their
prisoners safely back to their own lines. As the soldiers marched,
they picked up more prisoners along the way, including a
Lieutenant Vollmer, who had worked in Chicago before the war
and could speak English. York ordered Vollmer to line up the
prisoners and to order the others to surrender or else Vollmer
would be the next one "teched off." Vollmer blew a whistle,
signaling the remaining men to drop their arms. The group
headed back to the front, with Vollmer in the lead; York right
behind him, with his Colt in the small of his back; plus the other
officer along with two more German officers they'd picked up

on the way. Then came the three wounded Americans carried by POWs, the rest of the Germans, and the seven able-bodied American privates bringing up the rear.

As they approached the American lines, York was afraid he'd be fired upon because of all the German uniforms, and was relieved to meet a squad that Captain Danforth had sent searching for him. As soon as he saw them, York stepped in front of Vollmer to show his American insignia. Back at headquarters, the battalion adjutant counted 132 German prisoners of war and instructed York to take them to regimental headquarters because he didn't have room for them. Regimental couldn't house them either, and sent York on to division headquarters at Varennes, where he could turn his captives over to the French military police.

In Varennes York was ordered to report to divisional commander General Julian R. Lindsey. "Well, York," the general said, "I hear you have captured the whole damn German army."

"No, sir. I only got a hundred and thirty-two."

General Lindsey sent York and his patrol to the artillery kitchen for a hot meal, and then they walked back to their company headquarters. Writing that night in his diary, York ended his entry with reflections on his miraculous day.

"So you can see here in this case of mine where God helped me out. I had bin living for God and working for the church some time before I come to the army. So I am a witness to the fact that God did help me out of that hard battle; for the bushes were shot up all around me and I never got a scratch."

5

HERO

From the time Corporal York headed around the left flank of the American forward position until the time he returned with his prisoners and wounded was three hours and fifteen minutes. By nightfall of the same day, October 8, 1918, Company G and the 328th had taken the Decauville Railroad at the bottom of Hill 223. Though he didn't realize it at the time, Captain Danforth was able to lead his men forward largely because Corporal York had neutralized the machine gun nests that had been throwing deadly fire at them.

The next morning, York and the seven privates who had returned safely from their patrol reported what had happened. Danforth granted Corporal York's request to go back to the battle site with stretcher bearers in case there were any wounded left alive. A cleanup detail was already on the scene and had buried the six dead Americans where they fell. York walked to the spot where he'd stood firing at the machine gunners and saw that the grass was completely shot away. A canteen on the ground nearby had eighteen bullet holes in it.

There never was an official count of the number of Germans York killed. The first officer on the scene after York's battle, F Company commander Captain Bertrand Cox, said he saw "between 20 and 25 dead Germans." Another account reported "a dozen dead Germans and ten or twelve more pairs of legs sticking out of the bushes." By the time York returned on October 9, the Americans had buried the German bodies, so a final tally was impossible. Reports of abandoned machine guns ranged from twenty-eight to thirty-five to "more than thirty."

Army officials interviewed York twice over the next few days about the Decauville Railroad advance, and on November 1 he was promoted to sergeant. During the three weeks in between, York survived the longest stretch of frontline combat in his military career. The American advance was knifing through the Argonne Forest faster than ever, so fast that now the 328th wasn't even stopping to bury its dead. Retreating Bosch kept up their artillery fire and poison gas attacks. As he tried to sleep at night, York looked out across a nightmare scene of dead strewn across the battlefield, their faces twisted into the agonies of death and lit by flickering blasts from German shells. At Sommerance, York came closer to getting killed than any other time, when he was picking apples in an orchard and thought shells were falling far enough off not to be hazardous. By the time he decided he'd better dig in, it was too late. A shell exploded so close to him it sent him flying through the air, his ears ringing with the force of the blast. Momentarily stunned, he stood and walked away unhurt.

On October 31 the 328th marched out of the Argonne Forest and enjoyed a ten-day furlough in the town of Aix-les-Bains, where York took a motorboat ride on the lake and visited famous Roman ruins. He was there when he heard on November 11 that the war was over and the Armistice signed. On the fourteenth he sent a postcard home to Pall Mall. It arrived around Christmas. "Hello," he scribbled. "I'm OK Sending you a postcard view of a little of this country along the coast. It's a nice scene. Well, that's all."[1] He made no mention of Hill 223.

On Christmas Day, York marched as a color bearer in a grand review before President and Mrs. Woodrow Wilson in the city of Langres. The president and his wife both spoke to the large crowd. York enjoyed the day in spite of the biting winter wind. His only disappointment was that as a member of the color guard, his duties forced him to miss Christmas dinner.

In January 1919 York's battalion headquarters interviewed the seven privates who'd been with York on Hill 223 to see if the incredible story they'd been hearing was true. Could one enlisted man have actually captured 132 Germans? Considering the confusion of a foggy battlefield in high grass at dawn, the seven accounts were reasonably consistent, and most of them singled York out for special praise. Privates Percy Beardsley and Michael Saccina agreed that York fired on the Germans while the rest of them ran for cover or guarded the Prussian prisoners they'd taken at their breakfast. Private Joseph Konotski explained that York had performed "deeds of most distinguished personal bravery and self-sacrifice" in the face of heavy fire and the loss of all but seven men. "His comrades had lost hope but Sergeant York . . . rallied his men and closed in on the enemy, using his rifle as long as he could conveniently reach his ammunition. Then he resorted to his pistol, with which he killed and wounded no less than fifteen of the enemy."

On February 3, several officers, including Brigadier General Lindsey and Major Buxton, went back to Hill 223 with Sergeant York and had him walk them through what happened. The general asked him how in the world he could have done such a thing without being torn to pieces by enemy fire.

"Sir, it was not man power," York said. "It was divine power that saved me. Before I went to war I prayed to God, and He gave me my assurance that so long as I believed Him, not one hair of my head would be harmed. Even in front of them machine guns, He knowed I believed in Him."[2]

On February 11, Sergeant York was awarded the Distinguished Service Cross by General Pershing himself, who described York as "the greatest civilian soldier of the war." Later in the month, Pershing sent word to Major General George B. Duncan, commander of the 82nd Division, that he wanted more information on York's heroic act "with view of reconsidering this case for the award of the Medal of Honor." Military brass asked York if he'd be willing to make a speaking tour of American military installations in France, sharing his story and visiting with soldiers to keep up morale as restless troops counted the hours until they could go home.

Often traveling with Rev. Tyler, a chaplain from Milwaukee, York toured the French countryside, telling his story, answering questions, and talking about his faith in Christ. The YMCA sponsored many of his talks, where hundreds of soldiers and locals would crowd in to hear. York and Tyler established their base in Prauthoy, going out early in the mornings to speaking engagements, sometimes coming back that night and other times being gone several days at a stretch. Cold though it was, the pair occasionally traveled by motorcycle, which scared the Tennessee farm boy. "It was asking too much of God, traveling like that," he declared.

York was a huge success as a speaker. His experience as second elder in the church made him comfortable standing in front of audiences, and his heartfelt honesty made his poor grammar endearing rather than annoying. The sergeant continued what he called his "little talks" about fighting and faith in Bordeaux, where he was transferred on February 27. As word spread about this tall, redheaded sergeant who was in line for the Medal of Honor, audiences grew larger still. Troops appreciated anything that relieved the boredom of waiting to ship out for the states, and York's presentations were better than many. He usually started with a hymn or two, then a prayer, then his little talk about how his faith saw him through the battle of Hill 223 and how God enabled him to accomplish what he could never have done on his own.

Paris, the world-famous City of Lights, was coming to life again after years of war, and on March 26 Sergeant Alvin York stepped off the train to take it all in. "I liked Paris all right," he wrote in his journal the next day. "It was a right smart place. The Eiffel Tower [elevator] was not running at the time. I went to see it but I didn't climb it. It was tolerably high." He spent an incredible four dollars—more than a week's wages at the forge—on a ticket to the opera, "music with a lot of them stringed instruments playing together. I sat through it all right. I liked the orchestra, but I don't think I'd ever again spend four dollars to see another opera like it." He was also unimpressed by his ride on a Ferris wheel, when "the sky and the ground got all mixed up" and "I not only forgot the war, I done forgot everything."

One experience in Paris that the sergeant did enjoy was the honor of representing his division at the organizational meeting of the American Legion, held at the Hôtel Gabriel on April 7 and listing Sergeant Alvin C. York as a charter member. The next day he attended the formal ceremony ending the Great War, at the Palace of Versailles, and was presented to Premier Clemenceau and Marshal Ferdinand Foch, commander of French forces. He also spoke again with General Pershing, noting that all the Allied leaders were "religious men who believe in prayer." Later that afternoon, at the railroad station, he saw the queen of Romania, who, he allowed, was "a very good-looking lady."

By April 12 York was in the town of St. Silva, where routine duties included inspection with full packs, guard duty, and writing more letters home. He thought day and night about the hills of Tennessee and "my G. W.," to whom he sent word in almost every letter he wrote anybody. April 18, 1919, was Good Friday, and that day the 82nd Division held a historic review on the parade ground at St. Silva. There Sergeant York received the Medal of Honor from the division commander, General George B. Duncan. The citation, authorized by Congress on April 11, read:

> For conspicuous gallantry and intrepidity above and beyond the call of duty in action with the enemy near Châtel-Chéhéry, France, October 8, 1918. After his platoon had suffered heavy casualties and 3 other noncommissioned officers had become casualties, Corporal York assumed command. Fearlessly leading 7 men, he charged, with great daring, a machine-gun nest which was pouring deadly and incessant fire upon his platoon. In this heroic feat the machine-gun nest was taken, together with 4 officers and 128 men and several guns.[3]

As he presented the medal, General Duncan declared, "The commanding general takes particular pride in announcing to the command this fine example of courage and self-sacrifice. Such deeds are evidence of that spirit and heroism which is innate in the highest type of American soldier and responds unfailingly to the call of duty wherever or whenever it may come."

Sergeant York spent a quiet Easter Sunday at church, then as the guest of a local family for Easter dinner. Thursday, April 24, he was back on the parade ground with other soldiers, picking up cigarette butts. The ground had to look pristine because Marshal Foch was coming to the 82nd to present York with France's highest award. York stood on the reviewing stand as the division passed in formation. Then Foch stood in front of the sergeant, kissed him on both cheeks, and pinned the Croix de Guerre over his left breast pocket beside the Medal of Honor. Addressing the division and their guests, Foch said to York, "What you did was the greatest thing ever accomplished by any soldier of any of the armies of Europe."

York had still never mentioned Hill 223 to anyone other than his military superiors and the audiences at his "little talks." He seemed not especially proud of what he'd done. Those dead Germans were his brothers in Christ as much as his American friends were, and on the battlefield he'd said prayers for both of them. York had done what he had to do and wanted no special treatment for killing people out of necessity before they could kill him.

What he wanted more than anything was to go home. Finally, on May 10, he shipped out from Bordeaux to New York aboard the USS *Ohioan*. Again York was miserably seasick and didn't feel like "doing anything but lying down and being left tolerable alone. I would had got out and walked if I could have." On the morning of May 22, he stood at the rail as the ship sailed past the Statue of Liberty in New York Harbor. Looking into her face, he shared the sentiment of another soldier standing nearby: "Take a good look at me, Old Girl. Because if you ever want to see me again, you'll have to turn around."[4]

UNLIKELY MEETINGS

The United States Congress awarded 118 Medals of Honor to men who served in World War I. Generally, they received scant attention after an initial burst of public acclaim. The Medal was bestowed in a ceremony, there would be an article in the home-town paper, perhaps some speeches and parades, and that was as far as the notoriety usually extended. They (or the survivors of posthumous honorees) were left with the memories of their brave deeds, the thanks and admiration of those who knew their story, and a lifetime honorarium of ten dollars a month. (The average American wage earner in the spring of 1919 took home about one hundred dollars per month.) Like most recipients, Alvin York had no personal interest in spreading his story. If it had been up to him, he'd have spoken at some more prayer meetings after he returned home, enjoyed some good dinners, then receded into the historical anonymity his fellow honorees resumed within a few years after the war ended. The fact that the world ever learned of York's miraculous exploits is itself a miracle, the result of a chain of unlikely meetings and coincidences that, depending on one's point of view, were the consequences either of phenomenal luck or divine intervention.

The chain began with American painter and illustrator Joseph Cummings Chase, who was in France on assignment for *World's Work* magazine, one of many publications scrambling to satisfy the American public's ravenous appetite for war news. After the Armistice, Chase interviewed and painted a number of American generals, including John J. Pershing and dashing young Douglas MacArthur, already a general at thirty-seven, whom Chase described as "one of the most picturesque men in the Army."[1] Another of Chase's subjects was Major General George B. Duncan, commander of the 82nd Division. While painting Duncan's portrait, Chase engaged him in conversation, as he typically did to help his subjects relax as they posed. The general kept coming back to the story of a corporal in his command who'd captured 132 Germans single-handedly. Chase realized, "It was only by accident that the story came to his own commander, from the adjacent battalion some time later."

General Duncan told Chase he ought to paint York's portrait, too, and ordered the sergeant to report later that evening. Chase set to work, trying to engage York in conversation, but without success. The only comment he pried out of the modest Tennessean was when he asked if he was married. "No," York answered, "I was always kind of a mommer's boy." In his notes for the caption, Chase wrote that Corporal Alvin C. York from the mountains of Tennessee was a conscientious objector "who recovered from his pacifism sufficiently to kill with his rifle a machine gun nest of twenty-four Germans and capture 132," and that General Duncan considered this the "greatest single exploit of the war."

Chase crisscrossed postwar France and Germany to meet with his assigned subjects, catching whatever impromptu American military transportation was available. Sometime after painting General Duncan and Sergeant York, he was riding in the back of an army truck with George Pattullo, a reporter for the *Saturday Evening Post*. Founded by Benjamin Franklin, the *Post* was at the time one of the most popular weekly magazines in America. Chase repeated the story General Duncan had told him about Corporal York. Pattullo happened to be on his way to the 328th, and as soon as he arrived, he found Major Buxton and asked him about York. Pattullo then interviewed the sergeant, and went with him and General Duncan back to Hill 223 on February 3, where York retraced his movements for Duncan and other officers.

Pattullo was convinced he'd stumbled upon a phenomenal story, one that was all the more incredible because four months after the fact there was still not a word about it in the press. What a scoop! The practical problem was that from the time he submitted his article until it appeared in print would be six weeks, time enough for anybody to get hold of the news and put it on the wire service, robbing the *Post* of the impact of a breaking story. The reporter didn't want to risk putting time and effort into a project only to have the spotlight stolen from him. Someone might hear him interviewing the sergeant, or York himself might talk about telling Pattullo his story. The biggest risk was a leak at the military censorship office, which reviewed and approved all war-related stories for publication. Anyone there could tip off a friendly reporter, or say something offhand, or leave a piece of paper in the wrong place. Pattullo went to General Nolan, the officer at the top of the communications operation, and explained his dilemma. He wanted the story, and it would be great public relations for the army, but he didn't want the army to leak it before his magazine could print it. General Nolan explained that censors couldn't prevent other reporters from discovering the story, and couldn't hold their articles back if they submitted them ahead of Pattullo. But, he said, he could guarantee that no censor would leak his submission.

With that, Pattullo set to work on a long, detailed, highly descriptive and compelling feature article eventually titled "The Second Elder Gives Battle." In it he described how the corporal outfought the machine-gun battalion with his rifle and automatic pistol. "There were seven other Americans present at the fight, but it was York's battle and only York's. But for him not a man of them would have come out alive except as prisoners. In my estimation it stands out as the greatest individual feat of the war, not only because of the amazing things he did that day but because of the man's deep religious convictions and scruples."[2]

Pattullo asked the sergeant what he thought Pastor Pile back in Pall Mall would say when he heard that his second elder had killed so many. "What can he say?" York answered. "What can any of them say? 'Blessed is the peacemaker,' isn't he? Well, there was sure some stir-up in this country."

Describing the bayonet charge by six Germans, York recalled that they all "squealed like pigs" when he shot them. Did he get them all? "Yes, sir. At that distance I couldn't miss."

Pattullo wrote of standing at the battle site with York, looking at the shot-up grass and the fresh graves all around, and saying, "I cannot understand, even now, how any of you came out alive." The article concluded:

> York replied simply but earnestly: "We know there were miracles, don't we? Well, this was one. I was taken care of— it's the only way I can figure it."
>
> The last I saw of the big fellow he had only one worry— that he might be late getting home for the April meeting. They have a week of revival every spring in Pall Mall and he wants to be on hand; but he was gassed and greatly fears that his voice will be ragged for singing.

Without a leak, George Pattullo's feature made it to print in the April 26, 1919, issue of the *Saturday Evening Post*. The story created a sensation and made York a national hero.

Such was his fame that it penetrated even to the backwoods of Tennessee. Mother York received letters often from her son overseas. Since she never learned to read or write, she depended on Gracie, Pastor Pile, or another friend to read the letters to her. She always kept his latest one faceup on the corner of the mantel, where any visitor was welcome to read it. Carding wool beside her fire one spring afternoon, Mother York was interrupted by a visit from Will Wright, president of the Bank of Jamestown. The rare sight of his car in the Wolf River Valley attracted a small crowd of children and neighbors who scurried to the York cabin to see what was up. Wright opened a copy of the newest *Saturday Evening Post*, showing Mother York a big picture in the center of her son dressed in his army overcoat and standing in a dusting of snow during his reenactment on Hill 223.

The banker started reading aloud to Mrs. York and the others who crowded around her in the living room. When he finished the long article, he looked up and saw tears flowing down her cheeks. This was the first news she or anyone in the valley had heard of Alvin's heroism. As comments and congratulations filled the room, Mother York turned to Mr. Wright and said, "Read it again." He read it again, and five more times after that.

Sergeant York was astonished at the huge crowd waiting for him the day he arrived in New York Harbor after his voyage home. Reporters, photographers, and newsreel cameramen jockeyed for position at the pier in Hoboken, New Jersey, across the Hudson River from Manhattan, as they waited impatiently for the *Ohioan* to dock. A gaggle of wire service stringers and newspapermen chartered a boat and steamed out to meet York's transport in the harbor, circling the ship and yelling, "Where's York?" "We want York!" "Let us see York!" "Which one of you is Sergeant York?"

York figured he'd done no more than any other soldier would have done under the circumstances and had no idea he'd get such a reception. The ship had received a cable asking if he were aboard, but he hadn't thought anything of it at the time. Once he realized the people shouting from the boat and the crowd at the pier were waiting for him, the sergeant who had fearlessly faced down a machine-gun nest of Germans locked himself in a cabin below, frozen with alarm. After twenty minutes he walked down the gangway to a hoard of dignitaries, a band, and reporters shouting questions nonstop. The officers present saluted him rather than the other way around, a mark of respect reserved for Medal of Honor recipients. Bystanders scuffled for the privilege of carrying the sergeant's luggage to a waiting limousine.

"Are you really a conscientious objector?" one reporter hollered. "I don't approve of taking human life unless it is necessary," York answered, "but I considered it necessary."

"How did you kill all those Bosch by yourself?" another one shouted. "It was the hand of God that guided us all and brought about the victory," the sergeant explained.[3]

Crossing the Hudson by ferry, York refused at first to believe that all this commotion was for him alone, and not for the whole shipload of returning veterans. He traveled the streets of Manhattan through a storm of paper and confetti. The Tennessee Society of New York reserved a suite for him at the Waldorf-Astoria Hotel. Liveried bellboys raced to grab his field pack, blanket roll, and trench helmet. Glancing around his luxurious rooms, his eyes fell on a photograph of his mother that the Tennessee Society had had sent from Pall Mall. As an even better surprise, the Society arranged a telephone call from Mother York, who'd walked from her cabin to the nearest phone at Pastor Pile's store. Tennessee congressman Cordell Hull, born near the York farm and a member of the welcoming committee, ushered everyone—the "top hats and gold braid"—out of the room to give York some privacy during the fifteen-minute call.

The welcoming banquet at the Waldorf that night was lavish beyond anything York could imagine. Though the sergeant had never eaten in such splendor before, he seemed perfectly at ease all evening, sitting between General Duncan and a vice admiral from Tennessee. When someone asked him later how he knew which utensil to use and how to manage all the exotic food, he said he watched the person across from him out of the corner of his eye and did what he did. There were many toasts and speeches, ending with remarks from General Duncan recounting York's "outstanding act of gallantry."

Sergeant York rose from the table to respond. Exhausted after twelve days at sea (most of them spent miserably sick), the elaborate whirlwind welcome, and a long, late dinner, he spoke with simple grace. "I guess you all understand that I'm just a soldier and not a speaker. I'm just a soldier, but I want to thank the society and General Duncan, and I want you all to know that what you all have done for me is highly appreciated and I never shall forget it. Thank you very much." And that was all.

The next evening York took the overnight train to Washington, where, on May 24, he went to the Visitors Gallery of the House and received a standing ovation from the congressmen and visitors alike. He stopped at the White House, where President Wilson's private secretary greeted him and apologized that the president was away that day. When a reporter asked him what he'd like to do most of all, he said, "I'd like to go home and see my little mother."

Back in New York, he admitted he would enjoy riding the subway, and so the sergeant went on a special tour with a carload of dignitaries. Amid more dinners and parties, financial offers started pouring in. A magazine offered ten thousand dollars for his autobiography. A vaudeville impresario offered him a thousand dollars a night for thirty nights to tell his story from the stage. There were rumors of a fifty-thousand-dollar movie offer, and even a wild tale that a New York socialite had offered him a mansion, a Cadillac, and a stipend for life to father her child.

All Alvin York wanted was to go home. Heading at last to Camp Oglethorpe, Georgia, for discharge from military service, he asked during a stop in Chattanooga if he could get a haircut. He was ushered into a hotel barbershop, where the barber lowered York's head backward into the sink and went to work. When York asked what he was doing, the barber explained he was giving him a shampoo. York had never heard of such a thing. "That's the first one of them I've ever had," he observed. "They are not so bad."

The soldier's presence attracted a crowd. By the time the barber finished his haircut, the hotel lobby was jammed with people hoping for a glimpse of the war hero. Mayor Jesse M. Littleton of Chattanooga, who had been escorting York, led him from the barber chair to the mezzanine rail to see the people who'd gathered to welcome him home to Tennessee. To Littleton's surprise, the shy sergeant asked if he thought he ought to say a few words to the people. "Go to it," Littleton said.

This was the first public speech Alvin York made as a war hero. Up to now he had said almost nothing about what he'd done or how he felt. Something about this moment inspired him to set aside his quiet, self-effacing way and share his heart with his fellow Tennesseans. He thanked them for their welcome and their kindness, and added that the war losses in Europe had left the United States "the best Christianized nation in the world." In conclusion he said:

> In the war the hand of God was with us. It is impossible for anyone to go through with what we did and come out without the hand of God. We didn't want money; we didn't want land; we didn't want to lose our boys over there. But we had to go into it to give our boys and young ladies a chance for peace in the days

to come. Those boys who fell have done a great deed and a deed that will never be forgotten by America. Thank you.[4]

The soaring lobby echoed with the roar of applause and cheers.

On May 29, 1919, York was officially mustered out of the army at Fort Oglethorpe. The next day he took the Tennessee Central Railroad to Crossville, where every automobile in Jamestown—all six of them—waited to escort their hometown hero to his mother. Mother York, the rest of the family, and everybody else who could get there waited to greet Alvin in Jamestown. As soon as the motorcade clattered into view, the crowd started shooting off their guns in celebration. One neighbor had bought a new box of bullets for the occasion and fired her pistol into the air until it was too hot to hold.

After a round of handshaking and well-wishing, Sergeant York climbed up on the seat of the farm wagon beside his little mother, gave the two mules' reins a shake, and headed over the mountain for home.

A few days later Alvin described his homecoming in his final war diary entry.

My people from all over the mountain, thousands of them, were there to meet me. And my big redheaded brothers were there. And we all had a right smart time . . . I didn't do any hunting for a few days. I'm telling you I went hunting Gracie first.—

And then, when it was all over and I had takened off the old uniform of the All American Division and got back into the overalls, I got out with the hounds and the old muzzle loader; and I got to thinking and wondering what it was all about.

And I went back to the place on the mountain where I prayed before the war, and received my assurance from God that I would go and come back. And I just stayed out there and thanked that same God who had taken me through the war.

The End.

7

A VISION TAKES HOLD

The wedding of Alvin York and Gracie Williams was the biggest event in Fentress County history. Reporters had known the Tennessee hero was in love and jockeyed relentlessly for a scoop on when the ceremony would be. Midweek they learned that Alvin and Miss Gracie would be wed that very Saturday, June 7, and generated a flurry of articles about the festivities. When Governor Albert Roberts heard the news, he set his sights on performing the wedding himself. He'd missed out on the publicity in Chattanooga when the sergeant first returned to his native state, and York had declined the governor's offer of a statewide homecoming celebration on July 4. With a politician's instinct, Roberts well knew the star power of the most admired Tennessean in the country and saw the wedding as an ideal way to share the spotlight.

Probably York and Gracie had always assumed Pastor Pile would marry them. They likely would much have preferred their friend and advisor, a minister who had known them all their lives and had walked with them spiritually for so long, to a politician who scarcely knew York and had never met Gracie at all. But the Nashville newspapers reported that "a message was received Wednesday asking the Governor if he would consent to marry the young couple." Though the message surely came from the governor's office and not from publicity-shy Alvin, he and his intended submitted to the plan without a word.[1]

National wire service reporters estimated the wedding day crowd in Pall Mall at three thousand, while Governor Roberts's staff put the number at five thousand. Whatever the count, it was by far the largest crowd ever gathered in the valley. The day was beautiful and warm, and the wedding was held outside on a gentle slope near the river. There was a cluster of beech trees there, some of them so big that two men couldn't reach around them. At the end of the slope on the other side of the beech grove was a flat outcropping of rock. Alvin and Gracie used the rock as one of their meeting places, and they'd chosen that as the spot for their wedding.

The crowd filled the grove, their backs to the river, and faced the flat rock where the ceremony was performed. At York's request, he and Gracie stood looking out at the crowd, forcing the governor to stand with his back to thousands of voters. At the beginning of the ceremony, before reading the vows, Roberts turned to the audience and gave an impromptu speech about York's bravery and humility. The crowd responded with thunderous applause, after which the governor turned around and completed his official duties. York was dressed in his uniform, with the Medal of Honor and the Croix de Guerre on his left pocket. Gracie wore a new dress of light pink silk with red and blue flowers embroidered along the hem; two front pockets were made from silk handkerchiefs embroidered with American flags that Alvin had sent from France.

The ceremony was brief and simple. After exchanging vows, the bride and groom shared their first kiss as more applause and shouts of joy echoed off the valley walls. Everybody was invited to the marriage feast in a field nearby, where long tables made of sawhorses and wooden frames were covered with tightly stretched wire fencing overlaid with tablecloths. The cooking had started at daylight, and now the throng tucked into roast pork, chicken, beef, game, fresh and home-canned vegetables of every description, biscuits, cornbread, mountains of fresh honeycomb, and pies and cakes by the dozens. Women were in their Sunday best; local men had freshly laundered white shirts under their newest overalls, while the city folks wore their suits; children ran and hollered in every direction, shedding their shoes to climb trees, race through the grass, or wade in the river.

Mother York posed uneasily for photographers in front of her cabin, dressed as always in black from head to toe and an old-fashioned black sunbonnet, with the one festive touch of a white apron. "I'm getting old now," she protested, "and when a person gets old she don't look purty. I bet there's a lot of women are now saying, 'Wonder what that old woman wants to get her pictures in the papers so much for?' Bet they think I'm trying to show off."

During the celebration dinner, reporters kept asking Alvin how he could turn down the incredible offers of money that had poured in nonstop over the last week—one of the latest was from weapons maker Browning, offering twenty thousand dollars for an endorsement. Even if he didn't want riches for himself, they wondered why he wouldn't take them for his family or his church. He explained that every man had to lead his own life, and that his was in this valley with his people. Money led away from home and family and toward treacherous temptations. "Maybe if I had lots of money I'd get into trouble and be unhappy like many rich people I've heard about," he explained.

When the reporters pressed him, York quoted Matthew 16:26. "'For what is a man profited if he shall gain the whole world and lose his own soul?' I'll never give up my church and compromise myself with God for the sake of mere dollars."[2]

The Rotary Clubs in Nashville and Chattanooga jointly sponsored a honeymoon trip for the newlyweds to Salt Lake City, and Governor Roberts invited them to stop at the state capital on the way for a round of festivities. On Monday, June 9, Alvin, Gracie, Mother York, and some of their friends from Jamestown boarded a special car on the Tennessee Central in Crossville for the hundred-mile trip to Nashville, making fifteen stops on the way for Alvin to step out on the platform and greet the crowds. A sea of well-wishers waited for him in Nashville, parting slowly as his car crept through the crowded street from Union

Station to the Governor's Mansion, and then to the Ryman Auditorium downtown, where an overflow crowd had waited two hours to hear him speak.

Governor Roberts addressed the audience first; then Pastor Pile said a few words, after which the governor took the platform again to present York with a specially struck medal on behalf of the people of Tennessee. The honoree stood to speak at last, and the people rose as one, cheering, whistling, and stomping their feet on the wooden floor. His speech took less than a minute, starting with acknowledgment to the governor and other dignitaries of his award.

> Gentlemen, it is with pleasure that I can tell you how considerate Tennessee people are of me. I appreciate it highly. So highly that I cannot tell it as strongly as I feel it here [he touched his heart]. I have never met Tennessee people who are not proud of their soldier boys.
>
> The American army in Europe has accomplished the greatest victory known. They accomplished it with a will and with a spirit. It is the greatest army in the world today.
>
> Let's make this nation a more Christian nation than it is now. And while we shall always want to better our cbqlities and our nations, it is more important to better ourselves. I thank you.[3]

The next few days were filled with speaking engagements and other public appearances, including a baseball game, where he'd been invited to pitch the first ball to Governor Roberts. York had never seen a baseball game, but after a quick lesson pitched a solid strike to the governor, who dropped it. York spoke at banquets, went to vaudeville shows and a movie, and met with the Nashville Rotary Club, which had formed a committee to raise money to buy him and Gracie a farm. Asked where he'd like to live, he replied that he'd like to stay in the Wolf River Valley, where he'd been all his life and where all his family lived.

At last Sergeant and Mrs. York prepared to leave for Louisville, Kentucky, the next stop on their way to Salt Lake City. But Alvin changed his mind about the trip after a talk with Pastor Pile, who advised him that it was too worldly and tempting. Pile and York sent a telegram to their disappointed hosts in Louisville, explaining that the proposed honeymoon was "merely a vainglorious call of the world and the devil," and that they could "serve God best" at home.[4] Thursday, the Yorks and their party took the train back to Crossville, then a string of cars back to the valley, where they hoped for a little peace and quiet.

Alvin and Gracie moved in with Mother York and her younger children, and Alvin started building a house of his own next door. He went back to farming and hunting as before, yet scarcely a day went by without a stranger coming into Pile's store, asking for directions to the York cabin. Visitors arrived in a steady stream with more offers, and the mailman who rode over every day from Jamestown often had a whole bag of mail just for Alvin. There were letters pleading for money, asking advice, proposing marriage, describing investment opportunities. At first Alvin tried to answer every one, but soon gave up and tossed them in a big wooden box under the bed.

By the time Alvin returned to Nashville for a July 4 celebration (he evidently changed his mind and went after all), the commotion over his war experiences seemed to be winding down. On this trip there were no welcoming crowds at the train station or blocking the streets, no special railroad coach. While Tennessee's interest in their war hero appeared to fade, York still attracted a big crowd elsewhere. At the Methodist Centenary Exposition in Columbus, Ohio, his audience packed the auditorium and spilled out the doors. In typical fashion he had little to say, and didn't mention his heroic deed.

"I wish I could make a fine speech to you," he told his eager listeners, "but I am not a speaker. I'm just a plain mountain boy from Tennessee. All I have to say about the war in France is in honor of God, for without His help we would not have won. I live and practice a full salvation and I believe in continual prayer. While I was in France I prayed continually to God that I might come home without a scratch from the Germans, and I did."[5]

After the speech he toured the Exposition, where a cordon of soldiers protected him from the crush of admirers.

Alvin York was not an educated man, but he was an intelligent one. He realized that his notoriety gave him rare and valuable clout for whatever he wanted to accomplish. The question was, how did he want to use this powerful influence? Uninterested in riches for himself, was there a way that York could generate support for some worthy purpose while still honoring God? If so, how? And what should be the purpose?

During his appearances at Nashville and Columbus in July 1919, York had no goal or agenda. He went because people who wanted to see and hear a war hero invited him. It was sometime later that summer that Alvin York's thoughts and interests coalesced around the idea of using his fame to raise money for educating children in the hills of Tennessee. As a boy he'd had what he figured was the equivalent of a third-grade education, going to school intermittently for a few weeks or months at a time over several years. With no good roads into the valley, it had been hard for children to get to school, especially in cold or rainy weather. Almost no family could spend what it took to board their children for an extended period out of town. Besides, boys and girls alike had to start early pulling their weight on the farm; families needed their children at home to do chores they couldn't afford to pay hired help to do.

York developed a vision for a free, year-round school with the facilities and the budget to attract top-quality teachers. The building would be sturdy and warm, so children without coats or shoes could come even in bad weather. And it would be in a place where children could get to it year-round, or else it would supply free transportation to everybody in the valley. The Tennessee Railroad Commissioner, George Welch, was a good friend of the governor who had informally taken over as York's business advisor. He sorted through all the movie offers and concluded that no producer would settle for the religious slant York insisted on, and was trying to put a book deal together instead. Welch thought the idea of funding a school for the mountain children was a great one, and enlisted the Nashville Rotary Club in setting up a speaking tour to help raise money.

Rotary Clubs across the country signed on as sponsors, providing speaking venues, a bed for the night, and publicity. The first tour was a four-stage marathon covering the whole eastern half of the nation, west as far as San Antonio, north to Detroit, and east to New York and Boston. Audiences naturally would expect to hear about York's war experiences, but the sergeant insisted he wouldn't talk about Hill 223. He believed he was no hero, and that he only did what any other soldier would have done. He finally agreed to have someone else along to tell the story of his heroism in France, and then York would speak about his religious convictions and his dream of a school. Welch recruited his friend, Vanderbilt University professor Gus Dyer, to go on the trip and tell York's war story on his behalf.

The enterprise got off to a modest start in Chattanooga, where in contrast to his tumultuous welcome only a few months before, the theater was only about half-full. Sergeant York (though discharged, he continued using his rank, and did so for the rest of his life) told his audience he wanted to raise $150,000 for a series of schools in the Tennessee mountains. At the next stop, in Knoxville on September 15, the momentum was rebuilding as hundreds donated a dollar each for a reserved seat.

From there York and his troupe went to Birmingham, Alabama, where a big crowd was waiting when he pulled into the train station at 4:30 in the morning. Again reporters threw out questions about the war, and again York brushed them aside. "Let's lay off the war," he said. "I prefer to think of other things. The school for instance . . . We plan to make it possible for students to attend the school whether they have the money or not. They'll learn academic subjects part of the day and get practical instruction in agriculture the rest. There'll be a shop so they can learn trades if they want to."[6]

Alvin's speech had expanded from one minute to five, which a Birmingham reporter took down in shorthand.

My purpose in coming here tonight is not to talk about myself . . . when I came back [from France], I suddenly saw the need of education for the boys and girls of our mountainous country. I have learned as a result of my own lack of it just how much they will be handicapped when they grow up without it.

Everyone should be anxious to raise the standard in this country and there is just one way to do it: by religion and education . . . No other country in the world has a generation of young men such as we have today. And we've got to lend a helping hand to see that they and the coming generations are not held back by a lack of education . . . And it is to change that situation that I am here. I see the need of a school for those boys and girls.

Since I came home I have been offered a thousand dollars a day, but I remembered those lines in the little book that I always carry with me. "What shall a man profit if he gain the whole world and lose his own soul?" And I felt that if I accepted that offer, that if I forgot those boys and girls in Fentress County, I would be losing my own soul. So instead, I'm giving my time to help them. I'd rather see them totter to and from a good school every day than to have half a million dollars in the bank.

. . . I am not begging. I am simply pointing out the need of those people in the mountains of Tennessee and giving you a chance to subscribe what you will to its endowment fund.[7]

By the time York arrived in New Orleans on September 19, contributions and pledges averaged more than a thousand dollars a day. As the sergeant's train pulled in that morning, so many people crowded the platform that the police had to form a human wall around the perimeter to keep them from being pushed onto the tracks. Alvin and Gracie rode to their hotel in a coach drawn by four white horses. One reporter, after comparing York's feat with Sir Lancelot and Richard the Lionheart, observed, "You would take him for the sewing machine salesman who rides around town in a buggy . . . looking for whom he may interest on the installment plan . . . It's a comforting thought . . . that a man who has done what York has done should look like anybody else. And the comfort is increased by his acting like anybody else—only moreso."[8]

At the next stop, Houston, York raised $2,659 in one night. The group went on to Kentucky, Michigan, Chicago, and St. Louis. An audience member in Saginaw wrote, "There is something Lincolnesque about this character: simple, steadfast, self-sacrificing in its manifestations towards helping others. Such men, such character, form a mighty influence for national good; prove how sound at the core the great heart of the people is."

Though he shied away from battlefield stories, Alvin did comment for reporters on various other issues. In Louisville, hearing for the first time of union locals and closed shops, the veteran declared that if any authority "told me that I couldn't hire anyone but the man they said, why, I'd tell them all to go" and replace them with workers who "never heard of any other union except the union of democracy." He thought Prohibition was "a mighty good law" but opposed woman suffrage, which would become law within a year. He didn't believe women should vote because they weren't used to the idea and hadn't been thinking carefully about it. "They will many a lady vote wrong," he predicted, and there were already "enough ignorant men voters."[9]

York and his associates got home to Pall Mall in time for Christmas. In three months they'd raised about forty thousand dollars in contributions and had pledges for fifty thousand more. It was, the sergeant figured, "a good start."[10]

CHASING TWO MILLION

A lvin York had been poor all his life. Until now it hadn't much mattered because everyone around him was just as poor. The mountain people of Tennessee didn't think of themselves as needy or destitute. They were hardworking, God-fearing people who took care of themselves and their own. There might not be a pair of shoes for every child in the house, or a separate bed for each of them to sleep in, but they had all they needed, all they expected, and it was enough.

York's new status changed his perspective. Suddenly he was a national hero with big opportunities and big plans. He had been offered unimaginable riches, and many people assumed he was wealthy. Some of them, including several fellow veterans, were jealous of Alvin's celebrity. Neither Alvin nor anyone else knew how much longer the donations would keep coming in, but it was already more than York would have expected to earn in his whole life. George Welch set up the Alvin C. York Foundation to manage the money and handle the accounting and reporting that wealthy, business-savvy donors would expect.

All the notoriety and school contributions aside, Alvin still had to earn a living. He and Gracie moved into their new cabin next to Mother York, but he had no farm of his own. He could work her land when he was in town, though these days he was usually on a train or in a distant hotel. While he was away on fund-raising trips, the farm suffered because his brothers couldn't seem to keep up with the responsibilities on their own. They'd managed somehow while he was in France, but now that he was home and such a hero, they seemed willing to let their big brother take care of everything. York was not only a husband with a wife to support, but their first baby was on the way as well, adding an extra measure of responsibility. He was only willing to take travel expenses out of the Foundation coffers, and not a penny more. If he couldn't stay home to manage his crops and livestock, he had to find some other way to make money for himself. Alvin had very publicly turned down one fortune after another, then raised tens of thousands of dollars for his school, yet he had scarcely enough personal income for his family to get by on.

To make his private money matters even more troublesome, York worried day and night about the farm the Nashville Rotary Club had supposedly given him: a gift with unintended strings attached. The club had organized a fund drive to buy a farm in the Wolf River Valley and acquired three adjoining tracts of land totaling four hundred acres that had once belonged to Old Coonrod. It was some of the richest bottomland in the region, with the river running along the north side. Alvin had long admired it while farming his family's seventy-five acres on a nearby slope. On the first anniversary of Armistice Day, November 18, 1919, the club took title to the land for twenty-five thousand dollars, paying about thirteen thousand in cash and signing three promissory notes for the balance.

The club had hoped to own the land free and clear, but even after handing out pamphlet reprints of the *Post* article by George Pattullo as a reminder of York's heroism, they were well short of their goal. They went ahead with the purchase on the anniversary date, assuming they'd be able to raise the rest of the money soon. York fretted about the promissory notes. Even though he hadn't signed them and wasn't technically responsible for them, he felt burdened because the debt was for his benefit.

Tennessee representative Cordell Hull asked the House Committee on Military Affairs for assistance on York's behalf, without success. Commissioner Welch redoubled his efforts to negotiate a book contract for the sergeant. He'd made no headway with York on a motion picture. York believed movies were too worldly and immoral and didn't want anything to do with them unless they focused on Christian topics. Producers still didn't think a "religious" film would sell, and Alvin adamantly opposed a war picture. As he'd declared about so many other offers, he "told 'em all that this uniform of Uncle Sam's ain't for sale."

There was one slipup in the sergeant's avoidance of commercial publicity. He had lent his name, as well as Gracie's and Mother York's, to Wine of Cardui and Thedford's Black-Draught, remedies marketed by the Chattanooga Medicine Company. These were two of a long list of all-purpose health tonics aggressively marketed throughout the country. Made chiefly of peppermint oil, petroleum, vanilla extract, and alcohol (a popular ingredient during Prohibition), these miracle preparations could be taken internally or rubbed on the skin to treat everything from dandruff to arthritis to a host of feminine problems.

The Chattanooga Medicine Company built its advertising around endorsements by doctors, scientists, and prominent public figures, always including the fact that endorsers were not paid for their compliments. It may be that York was impressed that this was a Tennessee company, or that they made a point of saying spokesmen weren't paid. Whatever the reason, York signed statements endorsing both products, but when he first saw the ads in the spring of 1920, he was furious. The company ran a full page centered around him in his army uniform, the Medal of Honor on his chest. He wrote the advertiser on May 1, vowing "to see a lawyer and see if I cant make you stop." The company sent a representative to Pall Mall to smooth York's ruffled feathers, offered to make a contribution to the school fund, and promised to publish a special statement that York hadn't made money by appearing in the ad.

York waited impatiently at first to see this clarification in print, but soon turned his attention to more important and serious matters. Gracie's pregnancy had been a rough one. Home without her new husband for weeks at a time, she worried about him, about their baby, and about the financial strain the farm debt caused. When he was on the road, she wrote him two or three times a week. The picture her letters paint in April 1920 is of a brave young woman who is stressed, exhausted, and lonesome.

April 9: "Say darling I no that I have got the prettiest and best Husband in the World or ever will be and if you was to get hurt or killed I would go crazy. I hope you will soon have our farm paid for and that we won't haft to pay any attension to no one."

April 15: "I got a funny feeling when I was a Ironing today. I have been pretty bad today. I guess it was me working and carrying water. [Your brothers] . . . haven't worked but one day a piece sence you have been gone for you . . . I would rather see you tonight as for to have New York and all there is between here and there."

April 17: "Oh how happy I would be for to be in our house tonight so I could sit in my honeys lap and lay my arms around your neck and oh darling how I love you I would rather for that to happen tonight than to have this house full of gold."[1]

On June 5, only a few weeks after Alvin and Gracie moved into the cabin beside Mother York, their first child was born, a son. They planned to name him Alvin Jr., but it was clear from his first moments that his time on earth would be short. The boy had hydrocephalus, which the mountain people called "watery head." Excess spinal fluid collected around the brain, swelling his head, making the skin above his forehead pliable so that a finger left an imprint like a sponge.

The unnamed child lived four days, most of that time spent sleeping in his mother's arms. York sang to him often, especially his favorite hymn, "Onward Christian Soldiers." Alvin and Gracie prayed, and everyone in the valley prayed, for the boy's brief moments of life, sure beyond a doubt that they would see him again in heaven. He was buried in the cemetery at the Methodist church, where Old Coonrod Pile rested a few rows over. Whatever mourning and grieving the family did, they did in private. That was the mountain way.[2]

Within a month Gracie was expecting again, and York and Commissioner Welch turned their attention to getting Alvin's book under way. Welch chose a well-connected New York writer named Sam K. Cowan, counting on Cowan's reputation with magazine and book publishers to help sell the story. Cowan accepted the project for an unusually low advance of only six hundred dollars, paid by Welch, in exchange for 20 percent of whatever York earned from the finished product. Because York was so famous, and there was such demand for any information about him, Cowan anticipated a big jackpot.

The writer spent six weeks in Pall Mall talking with York, his friends, and family, getting a feel for mountain life, then went home to New York and his typewriter. Soon he realized this was a story he couldn't throw together in a few weeks for a big magazine spread—it was too long and involved—but still believed it had huge commercial potential. A sign of his confidence was that he turned down two much better-paying jobs, one at five thousand dollars and another at twenty-five hundred, to stick with the sergeant's story, even though he had to move his wife and two sons to a smaller apartment to get by on his meager advance.

As he finished his draft, Cowan made the rounds of New York publishers, expecting an enthusiastic welcome. He was surprised and disappointed to see that they now considered the York story old news. They felt that the public was sick of war stories and that the market had run its course. The *New York Herald*, which had long pressed York for a feature, turned Cowan down, saying the idea was stale. The *Saturday Evening Post*, publisher of the original York story, returned Cowan's manuscript unopened, commenting that they'd already run an article on the topic. Cowan and Welch hired a literary agent to help pitch the manuscript to book publishers, generating some mild expressions of interest that went nowhere.

Cowan delivered the manuscript himself to Funk & Wagnalls, which he considered one of the most prestigious publishers in the country, with their popular weekly magazine, the *Literary Digest*, and a famous series of encyclopedias. Funk & Wagnalls liked Cowan's book idea, prompting the author to write York that "to have Funk & Wagnalls say they think they can make a 'classic' out of it, is some pay for the blood I have oozed."[3] The sergeant was back in the national news in March 1921 when the *New York Times* reported on his financial woes. The war hero had "worked enough to kill a dozen ordinary men, but the season has been against him. His hay was practically burned up and other crops failed, and Alvin was left in the hole." He'd signed an oil and gas lease on Mother York's farm to try and bring in some income. Another opportunity that could have been a financial lifesaver turned into a waste of time. A weapons maker offered the sergeant two thousand dollars that summer to test-fire a new rifle, which he agreed to do until he saw men unloading camera equipment. York insisted on no pictures. Uncle Sam's uniform still wasn't for sale. They asked for one photo, and when York refused, they withdrew their offer, packed up, and left.

On December 9, Cowan reported he'd received an offer from Funk & Wagnalls, which all the parties discussed and negotiated until December 28, when a contract was signed for a royalty of 15 percent of the retail price, with York receiving three-fifths of the money and Cowan getting two-fifths. The deal reserved the right for York to sell his story separately to the movies, or to a magazine or newspaper as a serial.

Sergeant York and His People was published on April 20, 1922, backed by a major marketing push with 450 review copies sent to newspapers and other opinion leaders, and heavy advertising, including an ad on the table of contents page of the *Literary Digest*, with a circulation of 1.3 million. For all the support the publisher gave it, Funk & Wagnalls had advance orders for only three hundred copies. Booksellers didn't want another war book; the ones they had were being tossed onto the discount table at 75 percent off. Even so, sales took hold after a while, rose to a respectable level, and held steady.

It was a good season for Sergeant York and his family. His story was out now, told the way he wanted it told, and would start producing a royalty stream soon. He was gradually collecting the money to start building his school, and he and Gracie had welcomed a healthy new son, Alvin Jr., to the family. On Valentine's Day 1922 the young family moved into a beautiful new two-story clapboard home, a gift of the Nashville Rotary Club and one of the finest houses in the county. It had a telephone and a carbide generator that made enough electricity to light a bulb in every room. Best of all, from York's perspective, on May 18 the club retired the remaining debt on the land and presented the deed to York as "A gift from the people of America to the greatest hero of the World War."[4] The rich, level ground that Coonrod Pile once farmed was back in the hands of his descendant.

Now York could pour all of his energy into getting his school up and running. Originally he wanted to build a network of small schools in the countryside, taking education to the children who couldn't get to a classroom. When that proved too complicated and expensive, the sergeant and his advisors pursued the idea of a single school with dormitories, where the children could board; an elaborate agricultural operation, with barns and livestock; a woodworking shop; and a dressmaking shop. Including an endowment, the total price tag was an estimated two million dollars. An architectural firm in Knoxville designed a main administration hall with offices, classrooms, and a gym styled along the lines of a campus in England, its elegant brick walls and lancet windows trimmed in limestone, with a sixty-five-foot tower in the center.

York's fund-raising operation was reorganized as a non-profit educational corporation. He printed brochures to hand out on his tours describing the school and his vision, and high-lighting endorsements of the project. The sergeant still got far more invitations to speak than he could accept, and kept con-tributions flowing into the foundation bank account. But it was clear after a couple of years that the Alvin C. York Foundation could never raise two million dollars on its own. R. I. Hutchings, a Fentress County schoolteacher who sat in the state legislature, proposed that the state put up fifty thousand dollars toward the administration building. The state had never funded a high school before, and no one thought Hutchings had much of a chance. Perhaps inspired by the long odds, he spoke with unex-pected passion to his fellow lawmakers about "the poor, barefoot mountain children" with no chance for an education and no access to the halls of power to plead their case. Weeping openly, the legislature approved the proposal sixty-one to twenty.

The state appropriation was great news—far and away the largest gift to the foundation, adding another level of legitimacy to their plans, and likely to attract more big gifts. It also marked the beginning of a confusing and frustrating period for York and his friends. Government involvement soon led to a legal and financial tangle that fed political rivalries and turf battles, divided York from some of his strongest early supporters, and threatened to kill the effort entirely.

The Tennessee legislature established the Alvin C. York Agricultural Institute to run the school, separate from the Alvin C. York Foundation that had been collecting donations. The fifty-thousand-dollar state contribution was authorized on the condition that Fentress County issue seventy-five thousand dollars in bonds, fifty thousand to match the state amount for the York school and the rest to build a new elementary school for the county. W. L. Wright, president of the Bank of Jamestown, personally donated land for the York school site near the existing high school in Jamestown. The bond election passed by a wide margin. In the third precinct, which included Jamestown, the tally was 452 to 2. The local paper explained that of the two votes against, "one was cast by a woman and the other by mistake."

Agricultural Institute trustees were all Fentress County men who generally distrusted the wealthy, accomplished board of the Foundation, which included York's onetime traveling companion, Professor Dyer; former governor Roberts; former Treasury secretary William G. McAdoo; Methodist Episcopal bishop James Atkins; and Joel Cheek, who'd made a fortune marketing coffee named after Nashville's finest hotel, the Maxwell House. York was president of both the Institute and the Foundation, and both tried to get him on their side in their constant quarrels. The county government expected a say in running the school since they issued bonds to help pay for it, and so jockeyed for control with the state, the Foundation, the Institute, and their own school board, which was involved because their new elementary school was funded by the York-related bonds.

The first conflict came in deciding where to build the school. Will Wright wanted it on the land he offered, as did other Jamestown businessmen who stood to gain from a school on the spot. Others, including York, wanted it north of town on the newly named York Highway, a stretch of the Dixie Short Route that, though still only graded gravel, was the first all-weather road into Pall Mall. York wanted the northern site because it was closer to Pall Mall and because it had plenty of room for the barns, workshops, and other extras he envisioned.

By fall 1925, more than $110,000 was in hand, enough money to build the administration building, if only the Institute could decide where to put it. York waited patiently at first, repeating his reasons for wanting the school on the Pall Mall side of town, where there was lots of acreage, but the board was deadlocked, with three in favor of York's site and four for the Wright property. The longer the process stalled, the angrier York became. He'd spent five years getting to this point, and now the whole project was halted over petty bickering.

Legally York was helpless to break the impasse, but he had learned the power of public opinion. He announced a public meeting at the county courthouse in Jamestown, and told the large crowd that his school—their school—was being delayed by the Institute board. He said that if the people of Jamestown weren't willing to support him, he'd either resign from his own institute or build the school in another town.

On the spot, a lumber company offered him a thousand acres to build on their site. Allardt, a town down the road, volunteered six hundred acres and ten thousand dollars toward construction to put the school there. By going public, Alvin reminded his board of what this issue was truly about—educating needy children—and that he had the public support to do it his way. On November 30 the Institute announced that the school would be built north of town on the York Highway.

That still left the donations and appropriations snagged in red tape. York planned a trip to Florida, where millionaires who'd made their fortunes in land speculation seemed interested in his dream. New York financier John D. Rockefeller sent word that if the school could move forward without "becoming entangled with the state," he would "endow the school handsomely at the proper time." To follow these leads and fulfill his vision, York decided he needed financial independence from his own Institute. In December, he and Gracie took out an eleven-thousand-dollar mortgage on their new farm, and he prepared to start over from scratch raising money for his school.

While still considering whether to break completely away from the official organizations, York spoke to the men's club of First Presbyterian Church in Nashville on January 11, 1926. This was his first chance to gauge the reaction to the idea of building the school on his own. His plan now was to work with state chapters of the American Legion nationwide to raise his two million dollars. He talked about the importance of having the Legion in Tennessee behind him, and how they could work together to educate mountain children and teach them about

Jesus Christ. "When I die," he said in conclusion, "I had rather it be said about me that I gave my life toward aiding my fellow man than for it to be said that I became a millionaire through capitalizing on my fame as a fighter. I do not care to be remembered as a warrior but as one who helped others to Christ."[5]

A month later York met with the American Legion in Miami, where one of the state's most successful developers, Carl G. Fisher, pledged ten thousand dollars and others promised smaller amounts. York also had his eleven-thousand-dollar mortgage, and could borrow fourteen thousand more the same way if he wanted it. His trusted friend Arthur Samuel Bushing, a transplanted New Yorker who worked at the Bank of Jamestown, agreed to handle his books. When the Institute board kept dragging its feet on a building site, York resigned from the Institute, by way of a letter written by Bushing, "with deep regret . . . Hampered by the inaction of the majority of my committee and failing thereby to obtain that cooperation which is necessary, . . . I cannot in justice to the cause be further enmeshed and held back in the performance of my duty."[6]

On March 26, 1926, ten days after resigning from the Alvin C. York Agricultural Institute, York signed the charter of incorporation for the Alvin C. York Industrial Institute, with a board made up of close friends including Pastor Pile, and with Arthur Bushing as secretary. The new charter specified that board members must be "men and women whose character, achievements, patriotism, high ideals and good judgment prove their ability to help direct the affairs of said corporation." He believed having "Industrial" in the name was more attractive for fund-raising than "Agricultural."[7]

Jamestown and Fentress County realized that their infighting had cost them the school altogether, and that York was headed off on his own. In an unprecedented move, the county deeded the county poor farm, next to York's chosen site, to York "in order to lend him a helping hand, and to bid him God's Speed in his noble and most worthy undertaking."[8] The poor farm had 135 acres and a large two-story frame building, where the residents, their caretaker, and his family lived. The county bought another farm nearby and moved them all there.

Early on the morning of May 8, 1926, county residents began arriving at courthouse square in Jamestown. At ten o'clock, twenty-five hundred people, led by the University of Tennessee marching band from Knoxville, marched a mile north to a pine forest on a gentle hill. The first people arrived while the last were still lining up in the square. The 235 acres they marched to had been donated to York by Bruno Gernt, a wealthy lumberman whose family was the largest landholder and largest taxpayer in the county. It was the spot where York would start his school by building the administration hall. Until construction was finished, classes would meet in what had been the poor farm dormitory.

There was a series of speeches, a break for everyone to eat their picnic lunches, then more speeches. At last Sergeant York stepped up to the platform, said a few words, and turned over the first shovel of dirt as the crowd roared.

In spite of York's resolve to build his school on his terms with his money, there remained a knot of legal and financial confusion. The state appropriation hadn't been spent and would soon have to be renewed in the legislature. The money had been offered to the organization from which York had resigned two months before, and which was angered and embarrassed by his departure. The county judge who by law had to sign the school bonds refused to sign them because he hadn't been offered a seat on the Institute board. Finally, on September 3, the county school board formally joined forces with York's new Industrial Institute, consolidating the county high school with York's state-funded venture, agreeing to pay teachers' salaries and all expenses, and allowing the new board to employ its own superintendent and teachers "at any time it deems proper and necessary."

Three days later, the Alvin C. York Industrial Institute held its first day of classes at the poor farm. Across the highway a crew started clearing land for the new administration building, driving two new tractors donated by Henry Ford. York gave up the idea of building an endowment in the short term and concentrated on the one million dollars he'd need to build everything he had planned. He had mortgaged the farm the American people gave him and assumed he would eventually get the state and county money as promised. That left him hundreds of thousands of dollars short. After six years he still had a lot of work ahead.

FIGHTING FOR CONTROL

York's experience with Florida millionaire Carl Fisher was typical of the frustrations he faced in maintaining momentum for his school and holding prospective donors to their promises. After months went by without Fisher sending in the ten thousand dollars he'd pledged, Arthur Bushing wrote a letter asking when the Institute might expect his check. A secretary responded that Mr. Fisher had to conserve his cash at the moment, but would send secured promissory notes at 6 percent interest. After another wait, Bushing followed up asking about the notes and whatever collateral would secure them. Fisher's representative seemed insulted at the thought of promissory notes, saying that collateral would require too much paperwork and that Mr. Fisher had not "been in the habit of giving collateral notes and his unsecured note should be ample for any loan especially of such a small amount." Evidently the pledge was never paid.

By November 1926, two months after it opened, York's school was teaching an average of seventy-five to eighty children a day. The sergeant chaired a meeting of friends and advisors in Nashville to see if they could devise a way to proceed with the new building using private funds alone. Sales of *Sergeant York and His People* were steady but still disappointing compared to the runaway best seller everyone had hoped for. Funk & Wagnalls shipped cartons of them to the sergeant's speaking venues, giving copies away to anyone who donated at least six dollars. As other publishers predicted, the public was tired of war; the Roaring Twenties were in full swing, and the war seemed like ancient history. Furthermore, readers who were interested in York the hero wanted to hear about killing Germans, not about his religious conversion and life in the hills of Tennessee.

York's kitchen cabinet recommended he stay on the lecture circuit.[1] In December and January he went to Massachusetts, Missouri, and Kansas. Speaking at the exclusive University Club of Boston, he promised to keep school costs down by raising food for the children on his own farm. A Boston newspaper reported, "His message is one of inspiration and love of his mountain people. And once hearing him, no listener could doubt the high purpose which leads him onward in his mission." To a veterans' group he said, "There are no roads where I live. There are no railroads, but some of the beautifulest boys and girls that ever were. That's where I got my beautiful wife. But a third of them can't read nor write by the time they're sixteen. There's only one chance for a high school education there. That's the establishment of this school." His speech at the University of Missouri was broadcast on the radio. The sergeant handed out impressive brochures with endorsements for his school from General Pershing, Cordell Hull, Tennessee governor Austin Peay, and others.

Everywhere he went the praise was generous, but after deducting travel expenses the net return was far less than he and his advisors expected. His story wasn't novel or topical anymore, and the crowds were smaller and less generous. The York family's personal financial picture was even direr than the Institute's. No one knew the sergeant had mortgaged his farm and was barely scraping by. He and Gracie had three sons now—Alvin Jr., George Edward Buxton, and Woodrow Wilson—and Gracie's sister Kansas lived with them. Alvin also supported his mother. Friends and relatives assumed that since he was so famous, he must be loaded with cash. He made loans, cosigned notes, and put up collateral without ever turning anyone down or mentioning his own problems. A bad situation grew worse that winter when his barn burned to the ground, destroying an entire season's hay crop, many of his tools, and most of his cattle.

York decided to rethink his plan to abandon the public money. The state appropriation and the county bonds were still on the table, if only he could figure out some way to put them to use without the political bickering that had blocked his progress, and without losing control of the project. On January

26, 1927, he addressed the state legislature, asking them to nullify their previous appropriation and give the money instead to a new board. A private act proposed the next day failed, with some legislators arguing that this was a local matter for the county, that York didn't have the administrative skills to run the operation, and that he spent too much money traveling. Representative Robert Beck of Memphis said the sergeant had raised seventy-five thousand dollars and spent sixty-four thousand. When the sergeant's friends reintroduced the bill on February 1, it lost by a narrower margin.

Exactly two months later, the legislature considered the act again, and this time it passed, abolishing the original Alvin C. York Agricultural Institute and vesting its power (and appropriations) in the new Sergeant York Industrial Institute. The legislature's stamp of approval added to the festive atmosphere on Friday night, May 27, 1927, when the five boys and ten girls in the first graduating class of the York school received their diplomas from the sergeant.

Graduation exercises were at the First Methodist Church in Jamestown. The poor-farm building was far too small for the crowd that came to see the historic ceremony. Besides, the old Agricultural Institute board claimed the county had given it to their organization, not to York. The sergeant declared the building was his, and that if it wasn't, he'd hold his school somewhere else in the fall. When the Agricultural board balked, York and a crew moved every stick of furniture—desks, chairs, stoves, hardware, science equipment, supplies—out of the building and onto the York Highway right-of-way. The sergeant proposed that his school be consolidated with the state board of education, cutting the county school board out entirely. York eventually lost this battle; the eight students who graduated from the poor-house school in 1928 accepted diplomas headed "Fentress County High" from the county school board superintendent. The "official" York Institute at that point was a hole in the ground across the street.

Alvin revisited the idea of a book about his life to raise money. To reach the level of sales he needed, he'd have to write about the war after all. He decided to sell the rights to his diary, but the same publishers who'd begged him to write a war book years before now said they weren't interested. They also believed there wasn't enough material in the diary to make a book. Then, seemingly out of the blue, a stranger came to town who gave York a whole new level of opportunity for his military memoir.

Tom Skeyhill was an Australian writer living in New York, a war veteran himself who'd been wounded at Gallipoli. He first came looking for York in the spring of 1927, driving into Jamestown on "primitive and barbarous" roads that he insisted "did everything a decent, civilized road should not do." When he found his way at last to the York Institute office, up the back stairs of the Bank of Jamestown, Arthur Bushing apologized and said that the sergeant had just left for Florida. Bushing offered to answer what questions he could and to show Skeyhill the building site. A few months later, after exchanging several letters with York, Skeyhill returned to Fentress County, this time by rail. He took the passenger coach to Oneida, then rode the logging train that shuttled back and forth between there and Louvaine, where Bushing could pick him up and drive the last seven miles to Pall Mall. The logging train was all flatcars, so the occasional passenger rode in the caboose with the brakeman and the mail.[2]

Skeyhill arrived on a Sunday. Bushing took him to the Church of Christ in Christian Union where the sergeant was teaching children's Sunday school. York waved them into his circle and invited them to join in reciting Bible verses and singing hymns. After church the men went for a walk; then Skeyhill had dinner as a guest of Pastor Pile, who laid on "a sumptuous meal of beef, pork, chicken, beets, sweet potatoes, turnips, lettuce, homemade pie, and freshly drawn spring water." Following the big meal, Skeyhill went to York's home, where Gracie had recently given birth to another son, Sam Houston.

Skeyhill was convinced he could use the war diary as the core of an autobiographical best seller, and York agreed. The writer spent the winter of 1927–28 in Fentress County, living with Mr. Bushing, sitting around the stove in Pile's store, talking with the locals, tagging along on York's frequent hunting trips. York showed Skeyhill the diaries, explaining he had planned to keep them in the bank vault until his death, but that he would put them in a book if it would help get the school built.

Probably through talks with Skeyhill, York also decided to hire Famous Speakers in New York to schedule his speaking trips and negotiate fees. Almost overnight the bureau improved Alvin York's financial landscape, both what he had in hand and what he realized was possible. The first tour they planned guaranteed $500 a week for ten weeks. His fee was set at $250 per speech, or $350 for two speeches the same day. On February 6, 1928, York earned a $10,000 advance on his still-unwritten book; two weeks later *Liberty* magazine paid $30,000 for serial rights. Of the total, York got $15,000, Famous Speakers $15,000, and Tom Skeyhill $10,000. York's agent, Betty Smythe, loaned York the agency's portion on top of his earnings so he could repay a friend in Jamestown who'd paid off his mortgage note when it came due. He could still put away a substantial amount for the school.[3]

Tom Skeyhill's approach as a writer was completely different from what Sam Cowan had done, more action-adventure than historical narrative, and far more focused on the pioneer heritage and war adventures of "a mountain of a man, York of Tennessee. And like the mountain he has his feet on the earth and his head in the stars."

While his new book was under way, York fought to regain control of the poor house. His $750,000 lawsuit on behalf of "all school children of Fentress County and the Alvin C. York Industrial Institute" had backfired at first, forcing him to give up the poor-house building and transforming it into Fentress County High for a year. But the county action made the public so angry that the school board had to retreat, turning the building back over to York. The sergeant dropped his lawsuit, reclaimed the "Agricultural Institute" name for his own organization, and finally started construction of his administration building. The third school year started with an enrollment of more than a hundred.

York pared down his original grand plans for the new building, omitting the gym, side wings, and central tower for now, but still leaving a fine, large, two-story design with offices, an auditorium, and twelve classrooms. Every dime he needed was in the bank. It was a happy, productive period for the sergeant. He spent part of his time at his office in Jamestown or at the building site, part on the road speaking, and part in Pall Mall, plowing fields behind his two big Percherons.

Sergeant York: His Own Life Story and War Diary began its run as a serial on July 14, 1928, and was a tremendous success. York planned a tour to coincide with publication of the book version by Doubleday, but was sidelined by gall bladder surgery in Nashville. The sergeant had gained 75 pounds since the day of his draft physical, which he blamed on "plain country cooking," and now carried 245 pounds on his six-foot frame.

Later in the fall Alvin received enthusiastic receptions in Boston and New York. On top of the speaking fees, York's contract allowed him to collect donations for his school. Writing to Bushing from the Waldorf-Astoria on November 12, he excitedly reported, "Having some big meetings. Cant find sitting room for the crowds hundreds are turned away from my lexture. Cant get in buildings." Audiences passed around cigar boxes and stuffed them with money.

Even more excitement for Alvin York came on the morning of February 11, 1929, when the 108 students and five teachers of the Alvin C. York Agricultural Institute walked proudly through the front door of their new school building. Steam heat warmed every room, without cinders or smoke. There were electric lights, thanks to the school's own generating plant (there was no municipal power). York Institute had the only auditorium in Fentress County, and newfangled indoor plumbing the likes of which some children had never seen before. A barn served as a temporary gym, and since the generator wasn't hooked up out there, a second generator ran off the back wheel of a jacked-up truck.

Alvin York's dream was there at last in bricks and desks and chalkboards. Now he had to keep it alive. Completion of the York Institute put its namesake on a treadmill. He had to bring in money month after month to keep the school going while at the same time earning a living for himself. Political brushfires continued flaring up as jealous local leaders kept up a steady stream of criticism about the way York ran the Institute and how inept he was at business. The sergeant sold mineral leases on his land and opened a general store in Pall Mall, but neither of these ventures brought in any substantial return. Most years he operated his farm at a net loss.

Speaking and writing were the keys to generating the income York Agricultural Institute needed to stay solvent and keep expanding. Still there was cause for celebration. The day they occupied their new building, the school was in its best financial shape ever, with net assets of more than twenty-seven thousand dollars, including more than eleven thousand in cash. As York planned future speaking tours through his New York agent, Tom Skeyhill came up with another publishing idea. He rewrote the York story into an adventure book for boys titled *Sergeant York: Last of the Long Hunters*.

In August 1929, York looked forward to starting his first full school year in the new building when his local political opponents struck again. County school superintendent O. O. Frogge, Bank of Jamestown president W. L. Wright, the local sheriff, the tax assessor, the court clerk, and others filed a resolution with the state board of education, complaining that York and the Institute were acting beyond their authority, especially in promoting Christianity to the students. The state board hadn't acted by the time classes were supposed to start, so school was delayed for two weeks, then four. As the days dragged on with no resolution, the principal took a job elsewhere, and some seniors transferred to other schools to make sure they graduated on schedule. York enjoyed a welcome diversion when the Army War College invited him and other members of Company G to Washington to watch a reenactment of their battle. As he had ten years earlier, York received a standing ovation in the House of Representatives; then he returned home to try and get the Fentress County school board off his back.

Classes finally started on December 2 with York still in charge. But by then the sergeant had endured another crisis far more heartbreaking. Little Sam, nineteen months old, caught what seemed at first to be a fever and started having convulsions. It was meningitis, an inflammation of membranes around the brain and spinal cord, and the illness was fatal. The boy was in agony in his last days before mercifully falling into a coma and dying in his mother's arms. Sam's brothers were quarantined, so they had to watch the funeral procession from the house as friends and family followed the tiny, glass-topped coffin from York Chapel to the cemetery. Alvin confided to Tom Skeyhill that "Gracie will never recover from it." She was already expecting their next child: Andrew Jackson York would be born the following April.[4]

That same month, *Last of the Long Hunters* went on sale, and Sergeant York went on the road, speaking in North Carolina, Washington, New York, Illinois, Kansas, then back to New York. In December he wrote Gracie about plans for his birthday dinner, which was one of the biggest events in Pall Mall every year. "Have the boys to kill a hog so you can have fresh meat. And be sure to cook a nough to have plenty for every body. You could buy you a turkey if you want to and have it instead of a chicken. Just suit your self." York hospitality was well known, and anybody who was around at mealtime was invited to eat. Gracie and one or two hired girls cooked almost nonstop, feeding two or three seatings of guests and neighbors every meal. Fifteen or twenty at lunch or dinner was commonplace, everyone taking for granted that Sergeant York would foot the bill.

Baby Andy's arrival meant there were four boys in the house. The three older ones shared a bedroom upstairs, and Aunt Kansas had another second-floor room. The youngest child always slept with Gracie; she and Alvin had matching double beds in their ground-floor room. Mother York could have had one of the spare rooms upstairs, but preferred a pallet in front of the living room fireplace.

It took a while, but the stock market crash of October 1929 worked its way through the economy to York Agricultural Institute. As one consequence, the Tennessee legislature tried to shift responsibility for administering the school back to the county. The county sued, claiming York had taken the school away from their control and therefore the state should fund it. York was trying to raise more money for expansion and had never expected to pay teachers and operating costs. In 1931 the county stopped supplying school buses, and the state refused to pick up the expense. York paid for the buses personally until the state agreed to take over. Speaking dates at $250 a night all but disappeared, and Famous Speakers dropped York's fee to $150. Sometimes his hosts couldn't pay him at all.

Through the 1930s the sergeant slipped deeper into personal financial trouble as his income from all sources shriveled. More than ever, York was a soft touch for any friend or relative—and there were many—who needed a few dollars or a pair of shoes or a job. In 1934 the York Institute bus that brought children from the Wolf River Valley was taken out of service because the state could no longer afford it. York once again found a bus and paid to operate it himself.

When Franklin Roosevelt moved into the White House, York had confidence it would be a big boost to the economy.

He disliked Republicans in general and President Hoover in particular, convinced that Roosevelt and the Democrats would help the working man and get the country back on its feet. Roosevelt appointed York's old friend Cordell Hull as secretary of state, and in 1935 Hull petitioned Congress to make York a major in the army and retire him at a pension of $2,250 a year. The House denied the request, saying the veteran had already been "fittingly rewarded with the highest honor the government can bestow."

When word of Hull's petition hit the newspapers, writers editorialized again about why York hadn't accepted the fortunes he'd been offered years ago. Had he made only a few of the deals thrown at him the spring he came home from France, he would have had all the money he needed for his school and more. One commentator figured that two years in vaudeville would have done it. "Modesty is an appreciated trait as it is a rare one," this observer wrote. "But when a man is filled with an urge to benefit others, he should not be confused as to what is the personal equation and what is the best for his enterprise."

Meanwhile, the ongoing political cauldron at York Institute boiled over again. As chairman of the Institute board, York locked horns constantly with Henry Clay Brier, principal of the school and a friend of York's since childhood. Brier was obliged to do the school board's bidding, which York regularly disapproved of, insisting that it was his school to run as he saw fit. The final break came when Brier fired Alvin's brother Jim from the position of school janitor. When the state announced in 1937 that it would withhold a third of the school's next appropriation until the argument was settled, York appeared before the state board of education in Nashville and threatened to resign.

"It's my school," he declared. "I founded it and built it. I am going to expect the next legislature to take it out of the hands of the state board and turn it over to me, the man who founded it and fostered it without a penny of salary."

No doubt to his complete surprise, the board pushed back. York resigned, expecting another groundswell of popular support to force the board's hand, but the board called the sergeant's bluff and accepted his resignation. Futhermore, the board changed the qualifications for Institute board chairmen to say that whoever filled the post had to have a college degree. With the equivalent of a third-grade education himself, York was unqualified for the job.

In Arthur Bushing's final accounting of York's eight years and nine months as head of the school, the Institute had a cash balance of $1,331.97 on income of more than $76,000, including over $38,000 netted by York's speaking and writing. The sergeant had received $6,576.41 in salary and expenses from the Institute during those years. York considered forming another legal entity to try to retake control of the school, as he'd done once before, and asked Bushing to volunteer his services. Bushing couldn't afford to do that, but said he could work for $12.50 a month. York couldn't pay it.

Alvin could not afford to sit around bemoaning the loss of his school. By 1938 there were seven children in the York household. Betsy Ross, Mary Alice (named after both her grand-mothers), and Thomas Jefferson had joined the family. The sergeant took whatever speaking dates he could get for whatever fees he could negotiate, and kept up his other various enterprises. He also began keeping a closer watch on international news. In December 1937 a formation of Japanese bombers sank the USS *Panay*, a patrol ship sailing on the Yangtze River in China. The sergeant saw this aggression from Japan as a warning that they had their eyes on territorial expansion. Also, Germany under Adolf Hitler had been rearming for years in direct violation of the Treaty of Versailles that ended the Great War.

York was convinced that America's best move was to be well prepared for another war, and to be so strong that no for-eign power would dare to challenge her. He believed that all the men who participated in the huge Civilian Conservation Corps should also be trained as soldiers. (The CCC was a government project to put people to work building and maintaining facili-ties in public parks, campgrounds, and other similar places.) It seemed to this seasoned war veteran that his country wasn't paying attention to the growing danger overseas and wasn't preparing for what might happen if Japan and Germany grew even more ambitious. Writing to the New York *Journal American* newspaper, he warned of the consequences of inaction.

Did the United States gain anything from the last war? Yes, it gained . . . great prestige with all nations and was respected by all nations up to the time of the bombing of the *Panay* by Japan. And then we failed to get Japan to understand by meeting her face to face with armed forces, that our human rights and our property rights were the base of our liberty and freedom. Then we lost to some extent that prestige . . . We should not surrender any of the prestige or rights we now hold to any nation of dictators, because to do so would betray the faith of our forefathers who so bravely fought for our freedom and liberty, which we hold so sacred today. If Germany and Italy attack France and England, should the United States help either side? I don't see how we could keep out of war unless we surrendered our human rights and our property rights in the whole European country and bottled ourselves up in the United States. We should build up our army and navy to ten times its present strength. And we should fortify every foot of coastline we have, and fortify it strong. And we should start our factories to making [tens of thousands of] airplanes . . . For in my opinion, the better we are prepared to fight, the less trouble we will have with other powers.[5]

Having lost money for years as a farmer, York researched the prospects for cattle breeding and decided to buy some Hereford cattle in Texas. He managed to scrape together enough money for the cows but couldn't afford a train ticket. He hitched a ride to Texas and rode back with his animals in the cattle truck. Still, the financial struggle continued. A company that had leased mineral rights from him sued for sixty thousand dollars, claiming he'd violated their contract. York was acquitted; losing the case would have bankrupted him. When the generator at his house caught fire and the sergeant couldn't afford to have it fixed, his family went back to kerosene lamps.

In June 1939 York took his first trip to California to attend the Golden Gate International Exposition in San Francisco and the state fair in Sacramento. The June 10 issue of *Time* magazine ran an unflattering photo of the hefty sergeant stuffed uncomfortably into his army uniform. The brief accompanying article described him as "fat, arthritic, and peace-loving."[6]

A month later he was on the opposite coast, at the New York World's Fair for Tennessee Day on July 22. After years on the stump, York had matured into a compelling and effective speaker. To a large crowd at the fair and a network radio audience, he underscored the principles he believed had made his state and his nation great. "The spiritual environment and our religious life in the mountains have made our spirit wholly American, and that true American pioneer spirit still exists in the Tennessee mountains . . . God save America and strengthen our arms. And lift up the hands that hold up our flag, Old Glory, that she, the Stars and Stripes, wave over the land of the free and the home of the brave."[7]

Back in Pall Mall the next week, Alvin York registered a charter of incorporation for the Alvin C. York Bible School. Teaching Christianity had been one of the main points of friction (other than politics) between York and the county school board. York remained a figurehead at the Agricultural Institute, handing out diplomas and speaking at every graduation, and still loved the school even though he had no meaningful role there. But at the same time, the dream of the school he had originally envisioned, founded on Christian principles, remained unfulfilled. Also that summer he took three steps he hoped would give him some financial relief: he applied for an old age pension for Mother York, applied for veteran's benefits for himself, and—for the first time since his marriage—he applied for a job.

Mother York's pension request was denied, the form letter said, because "your children are able and willing to provide you with the necessities of life." The Veteran's Administration asked York for detailed personal financial records, which he didn't have and had never kept. Arthur Bushing had always managed his business affairs, but he'd never maintained any personal financial files.

The good news came with step three: the sergeant secured a job with the Civilian Conservation Corps. He was put in charge of a work crew at a park in Crossville, Tennessee, building stone walls, entryways, roads, and picnic tables. But this providential employment and its regular paycheck lasted only from October 1939 to April 15, 1940, the day Alvin took off in an entirely new and unexpected direction. Hollywood came knocking again, and this time Sergeant York opened the door.

GOING HOLLYWOOD

Alvin York thoroughly enjoyed his job with the CCC. Though there were unavoidable annoyances of routine paperwork and petty government politics, York spent most of the time outdoors, supervising a crew of eager young men grateful to be employed, even if a lot of the work seemed to be hauling endless loads of rock and gravel. Crossville was only fifty miles from Pall Mall, straight down York Highway and the Dixie Short Route, so York could go home often to see his mother and monitor his various business interests. Some of the camps, including Crossville, were slated to close on March 31, 1940. York applied for a job with the Veterans Administration hospital in Murfreesboro, hoping to land a new position before his old one was discontinued. The CCC reversed itself and decided not to close Crossville after all, but York pursued his application with the VA anyway.

One late February day, York received a telegram forwarded

119

from Pall Mall. The sender requested a meeting with the sergeant to discuss "a historical document of vital importance to the country in these troubled times." The same person had asked to meet with him before and York had turned him down flat. But circumstances were different now.

The telegram was from Jesse Lasky, until recently the producer of the CBS network radio program *Gateway to Hollywood*. Lasky had been in show business for more than thirty years, sometimes on top of the world and other times scrambling to keep his career afloat. He started out playing the cornet in Alaskan saloons after failing to strike it rich during the 1898 gold rush. Later he moved into managing business affairs for vaudeville acts. Within a few years he was business agent for the biggest stars on the stage, including Al Jolson and Mary Pickford. From there he climbed to the top of the theatrical ladder as a Broadway producer, whose lavish revues were some of the most popular of the season year after year. Unfortunately, Lasky spent so much money on knockout shows that he went bankrupt. Three years later he entered the fledgling motion picture business, forming Paramount Pictures with his brother-in-law, Samuel Goldwyn (who hadn't yet changed his anglicized name from Goldfish; it was originally Schmuel Gelbfisz), Adolph Zukor, and Cecil B. DeMille.[1]

Lasky was forced out of Paramount in 1932 when, in a repeat of his Broadway business, he kept spending top dollar on movie production even as profits plummeted during the

Depression. He freelanced at Twentieth Century Fox and at United Artists, then headed the radio project with CBS. In 1939 *Gateway to Hollywood* went off the air, and Jesse Lasky, nearing sixty and seemingly past his prime, needed a job. He had been one of the thousands of cheering New York bystanders who watched Sergeant York's welcome-home parade in the spring of 1919. He'd offered York a movie contract then and several times over the years since, but the sergeant always turned him down.

Desperate for a hit, Lasky contacted York again, hoping world events would convince him to change his mind. Europe was at war, and York, along with many others, thought America should send supplies and weapons to help the British. Others, including the famous aviator Charles Lindbergh, were strongly noninterventionist, meaning they considered the war none of America's business and not worth the commitment of American resources. Lasky thought he could convince York that his story on film now, focusing on patriotism, bravery, and the price of freedom, would sway popular opinion to support aid for Britain and France.

Lasky was right. After refusing even to discuss a movie for twenty years, York was willing to think about it in the light of promoting pro-interventionism. The sergeant bristled at the thought of Hitler mowing down one European city after another, seemingly unopposed. The Nazis appeared ready to gobble up the whole continent as America stood by and watched. York believed his story would show the power of faith in battle

and stir America's deeply rooted patriotism and love of freedom to the point that the people would step up and help their
failing allies.

Another immediate reason for making a deal with Hollywood was that it would give him the money he needed to build
his Bible school. It would also enable York to build dormitories and other long-planned buildings at York Institute, which
he still generously supported despite losing his battle for control. As Lasky had hoped, York agreed to talk face-to-face.

The two met at a Crossville hotel on March 9, 1940. Lasky
flew from Los Angeles to Nashville, with stops in Phoenix and
Dallas, then took a taxi more than a hundred miles to Crossville.
Lasky alerted the newspapers, who had photographers staked
out to snap the sergeant's photo as soon as he walked through
the door. Though they had corresponded for years, they'd
never met. At last, here they were, the sergeant in khaki work
clothes fresh from his job at the CCC, and Lasky in his custom-
tailored suit.

York drove his visitor to Jamestown for a look at the
Institute, then to Pall Mall to meet his family and to see the
Bible school site, set between York's home and his mother's
old farm. They discussed business some that day, and again at
the Hermitage Hotel in Nashville on March 14, when they met
with their lawyers. The Associated Press was already reporting
that a movie on the life of the famous Sergeant York was in the
works and that York would serve as technical advisor. Lasky
reportedly offered York twenty-five thousand dollars for the

rights to his story, but the sergeant wanted fifty in order to build his Bible school.

When Lasky handed York a contract, the sergeant glanced at it and passed in on to his lawyer. It was too long and complicated, the sergeant said. He wanted something simple and straightforward, believing that making a movie deal should be as easy as buying a mule: the only important thing was the honesty of the traders. After twice postponing his return to California, Lasky left without a contract but was back at the Hermitage in less than a week. Negotiations continued for two more days, with Lasky jockeying for maximum leverage and financial gain and York holding out for what he thought he needed for the Institute and Bible school. Once in a while York would leave the negotiations and disappear down the hall. Curious after it had happened several times, Lasky walked down to York's hotel room and knocked. Hearing no answer, he opened the door softly and saw the sergeant on his knees beside the bed, in prayer. Lasky closed the door and went back to the conference table to wait.

Facing the prospect of a second fruitless trip to Tennessee, Lasky was staring idly out the hotel window at the state capitol when he had an idea. He excused himself and went to the lobby, where he called Governor Prentice Cooper, whom he knew was a big proponent of the movie idea, and told him York had agreed to do the picture. Cooper suggested (as Lasky knew he would) that they sign their contract in the governor's office, but that they come right away because he was leaving for the weekend. On his way back upstairs, Lasky tipped a bellboy to come to the room in five minutes and say Lasky had a call from the governor.

When the message came, Lasky left the room again and returned saying the governor had invited them to sign their contract in his office right away. When York's attorney insisted his side wasn't ready to sign, Lasky suggested they sign a dummy contract for the governor and the news photographers. If they made a deal before Lasky returned to Los Angeles, the newspapers would have their photo—great publicity for the movie. If they didn't make a deal, the papers could throw the picture away.

They arrived at the governor's office and explained the situation. "Then you might as well sign this bill I can't get through the legislature," the governor said, taking an official-looking document out of his desk. "I'd like to see some use made of it." Surrounded by photographers, the three posed; then York and Lasky walked back to the hotel to continue their talks. Later in the day they heard newsboys on the sidewalk, crying, "Extra! Extra! Contract signed for Sergeant York movie!" As far as the public knew, the deed was done. Though he still wasn't completely satisfied with the deal, the sergeant signed. He would get five hundred dollars a week as a technical consultant, plus a percentage of gross movie receipts beginning at 4 percent for anything over three million dollars and increasing to a maximum of 8 percent of everything over nine million. Lasky gave York a personal check for twenty-five thousand dollars as an advance on his profits, with a promise of an additional twenty-five thousand later in the year.

In Lasky's view, the only actor to play Sergeant York was Gary Cooper. Lasky knew "Coop" was York's first choice, too, though York had no official say in the matter. Lasky had already approached Cooper with the idea, and the actor had turned him down. Coop was hoping his next film would be an adaptation of the novel *For Whom the Bell Tolls* by his good friend and hunting buddy Ernest Hemingway. Also, he felt too much pressure at the thought of portraying an international hero who was still alive. At the Nashville airport on his way back to California, Lasky sent Cooper a telegram: "I have just agreed to let the motion picture producer Jesse L. Lasky film the story of my life, subject to my approval of the star. I have great admiration for you as an actor and as a man, and I would be honored, sir, to see you on the screen as myself." He signed the cable "Sergeant Alvin C. York." His first morning back in California, Lasky borrowed twenty-five thousand dollars on his life insurance to cover the advance check he'd given York.

In a little more than two weeks, Lasky had sold his contract with York to Warner Bros. for forty thousand dollars and a salary as producer of fifteen hundred dollars a week with forty weeks guaranteed, plus a percentage of the gross starting at 20 percent and ramping up to 25. It was a very handsome return on his investment.

Lasky and the studio invited York out west for a visit. He arrived at the Los Angeles railroad station aboard the Santa Fe

Super Chief on August 22, 1940. (The sergeant had flown once years before in the Everglades and was unnerved by it. He never flew again.) Lasky wanted to be seen around Hollywood with his hero and also hoped York could convince Gary Cooper to play him in the film. Warner Bros. mounted a festive welcoming ceremony, including a committee from the Veterans of Foreign Wars, local Medal of Honor winners, the American Legion accordion ensemble, a formal welcome on the steps of city hall, and luxury accommodations at the Hotel Roosevelt in Hollywood.

The next day Lasky invited York to his house, where the host enjoyed scotch and a cigar while the sergeant drank tea. Then the two walked across the street to Gary Cooper's house. The star answered the door in his socks, and the three sat down to chat. Lasky tried and failed to get a conversation going, producing only what he later remembered as "huge blobs of dead silence." At last he mentioned York's gun collection, and suddenly Coop and York were off and running about guns and hunting. Coop seemed to be warming to the idea of playing York's character in Lasky's film. But even if Cooper said yes, the problem remained that Lasky had made his deal with Warner Bros. and Cooper was under contract to Samuel Goldwyn, Warner's archrival, Lasky's former business partner and brother-in-law. Lasky himself had muscled Goldwyn out of Paramount years before the other partners had shown Lasky the door. Warner's would have to negotiate with Goldwyn for Cooper's services. York returned to Tennessee with the question still hanging of who would portray him.

Meanwhile, the studio had hit a snag in dealing with York's seven other squad members. Lasky's contract with York specified that while most of the story could be fictionalized, the account of the battle on Hill 223 had to be historically accurate. York's seven buddies had to appear as characters in the film, which meant Warner Bros. had to get permission from each one to use his identity. A couple of them had long resented York's notoriety. Otis B. Meritthew, who had enlisted under another name so his mother wouldn't know he had gone to war, wrote the studio to say he and the others had never signed affidavits affirming York's heroic feat and that "if they signed any papers in France they thought that they were signing a 'supply slip' for a suit of underwear or some such thing."[2]

The studio unintentionally made matters worse by negotiating separately with each person. Captain (later Major) Danforth, whose character would also appear in the film, asked for $1,500 and got it. Otis Merrithew, unhappy though he was, signed his permission form for $250. Most of the other squad members signed for $20 and were glad to have it; one signed for $5. When a story came out on the wire services that each squad member was paid $250, the men who had made $20 started calling newspapers and American Legion posts, complaining that they'd only gotten a fraction of that. True, it was all they'd asked for, but now they felt cheated. Warner Bros. quickly agreed to pay each man the difference between his original amount and $250, then sent their checks to American Legion offices for delivery, giving that organization a publicity boost.

Lasky asked Howard Hawks to direct the film. Hawks had just started shooting *The Outlaw* for Howard Hughes, but agreed to consider doing Lasky's picture next as a favor, since Lasky had given Hawks his first job in the movie industry. Hawks also thought he could convince Gary Cooper to play York, and got Coop on the phone in Lasky's office.

"Coop, didn't Lasky give you your first job?" Cooper admitted that, yes, Lasky hired him for his first screen role, in the 1925 silent hit *Wings*. "Well, he's broke, he's got the shakes, he needs a shave, and he's got a story that I don't think it would hurt either one of us to do." After the conversation continued for a few minutes, Hawks said, "Look, Coop, we have to talk about this."

"What is there to talk about?" Coop asked. "You know we're gonna do it."

The next hurdle was getting Samuel Goldwyn to loan Coop for the picture. In exchange for his biggest star, Goldwyn wanted the biggest star at Warner Bros., Bette Davis. Warner distributors and theater owners howled in protest at the news. They strongly opposed loaning out Bette Davis to the competition; surely somebody else could play Sergeant York.

Warner Bros. had mentioned or considered several top stars as possibilities, including Spencer Tracy, James Cagney, and Henry Fonda. Hesitant to run roughshod over their distribution network, the studio reconsidered whether there wasn't anyone else who could handle the part. They even screen-tested one of their own up-and-coming feature players, a handsome, dark-haired young actor named Ronald Reagan. In the end, the producers traded Bette Davis for Cooper. Lasky was delighted with the transaction and also relieved. Soon he would owe Sergeant York his second twenty-five-thousand-dollar advance, whether the picture was under way or not.

Hawks didn't wait to finish *The Outlaw* after all. Ten days into the project, he resigned over differences with his producer, telling Howard Hughes to direct it himself. *Sergeant York* could start shooting as soon as Cooper returned from his guaranteed one-month break between films. At long last, Lasky's production began on February 3, 1941, on Sound Stage 6 at the Warner Bros. studios in Burbank. They were rolling even though the final script still wasn't finished, and Hawks got pages of new dialogue and changes every day. Screenwriters kept working to balance the war story with York's spiritual and patriotic themes. They'd also had to develop the character of a fictitious uncle to replace Gracie's father, who refused permission to use his name at any price, claiming movies were sinful. The last major role to be cast was Gracie. Lasky wanted a sexy siren in the part (his first choice was Jane Russell), but others convinced him that York would never consent to that. York also insisted that whoever played Gracie could not be a smoker. The studio ended up casting an ingenue named Joan Leslie, who learned the news during her sixteenth birthday party. Cooper was thirty-nine, and it took them a while to get comfortable with the idea of a romantic relationship on-screen.

Most of the movie was filmed at Sound Stage 6. Battle

scenes were shot by a second unit in a barley field in the Simi Valley, where tractors, dump trucks, and dynamite re-created the Argonne battle site. The scene of York being awarded the Medal of Honor was shot at Los Angeles city hall, using a genuine medal borrowed from the adjutant general of the army. The production concluded on May 3, coming in at just under $1.4 million. The studio hoped to schedule a New York premiere for July 4. York and Lasky waited impatiently to see whether their dreams would come to life—Lasky's of boosting his sagging career, and York's of finishing the schools he had struggled twenty years to complete.

11

MAMMON

lvin York arrived at New York's Pennsylvania Station on July 2, 1941, to attend the most widely anticipated movie premiere of the year. Above the Astor Theater on Broadway, one of the biggest electric signs ever built—four stories high and half a block long—featured two alternating images of Gary Cooper, a mountaineer holding a muzzle loader and a soldier sighting down his infantry rifle. Underneath, lights spelled out huge letters reading, "Gary Cooper in *Sergeant York.*" The last Hollywood movie with so many advance ticket sales had been *Gone with the Wind.*[1]

Reporters surrounded York at the station, asking not about the film but about what he thought America should do to help Europe. Paris had fallen to the Nazis, and London was enduring devastating night bombing by the *Luftwaffe.* The United States was sending aid across the Atlantic, but German U-boats were sinking the cargo ships. York declared American merchant ships should sail in armed convoys, even if it jeop-ardized U.S. neutrality. Reporters reminded York that former President Hoover was noninterventionist. "That's why he's ex-president," York quipped. York, Cooper, and Lasky met at Lasky's apartment in the Ritz Towers, then took a limousine to the theater. During the ride, Lasky and York reminisced about York's ticker-tape parade down the same street twenty-two years before.

Sergeant York was a smash hit. *Variety* figured it would be the biggest moneymaker of the year. Influential columnists and critics of the day hailed it as a masterpiece. Walter Winchell wrote that it was "a Yanky Doodle Dandy that I encourage everyone to see." Dorothy Kilgallen called it "one of the greatest entertain-ments of all time." Louella Parsons declared *Sergeant York* "one of the finest pictures of any year."

At a luncheon the next day, sponsored by the Tennessee Society, York reaffirmed his conviction that America had to give Europe a helping hand, but that the help didn't require putting American lives at risk. "England does not need our manpower over there," he told reporters. "What she needs is our manpower over here, producing planes and guns and tanks and boats." York also insisted he didn't want war with Germany. "No one can possibly hate war as much as a soldier who has tried to catch his breath with the mud of the trenches caked on his face."

York and Gracie, their son Woodrow, and Arthur Bushing's son, Arthur, arrived for the Washington, D.C., premiere on

July 31 to an elaborate reception from Tennessee governor Prentice Cooper, both Tennessee senators, the undersecretary of war, the chairman of the senate military affairs committee, and York's old division commander, General Duncan, now retired and living in Kentucky. The Veterans of Foreign Wars, American Legion, Boy Scouts, U.S. Marine Band, and a long list of other organizations joined in the massive welcoming ceremony. Afterward the sergeant, Gracie, the two boys, and Lasky were whisked off to the White House and presented to President Roosevelt, who congratulated York on the movie.[2]

It was Sergeant York day at the Capitol, and so many legislators wanted to speak to him that he missed a visit to the House Chamber, where he was scheduled to open the day's session with a prayer. After an evening reception, York got in a car for the short ride to the theater, and watched bemused as a crowd of dignitaries—the men in black ties and ladies in long dresses—walked and trotted along beside him the whole way. After the showing, Lasky sent a telegram to Warner Bros. calling it the "greatest evening I have ever witnessed in a theater. Notices and publicity sensational."

The third and final premiere was in Nashville on September 18. Gracie attended again, and Alvin Jr. and Pastor Pile came as well. The pastor had been against the movie at first, but had come around to believe that this film could make him an instrument in God's hands to help Sergeant York toward "a nobler, broader life." He added that he hoped the film would lead audiences "to that beautiful city from which there is no return."

From an artistic standpoint Pile declared the "speaking part is pretty good. But goodness," he exclaimed, "I was never as ugly as that fellow" (three-time Oscar winner Walter Brennan, who played Pile on-screen).

York's squad member Otis Meritthew complained again publicly that York was getting far more press and credit than he deserved, and author Sam Cowan groused that Warner Bros. had plagiarized his work. But these criticisms were lost in a nationwide swell of approval and popularity as *Sergeant York* became a box office success. On top of his advance payments from Lasky and the hope of more money to come, Sergeant York gained a powerful national platform for his pro-interventionist position. The most compelling speech he ever gave on the subject, and arguably his most moving speech ever, had been at the Tomb of the Unknown Soldier at Arlington National Cemetery in Washington on Memorial Day, May 30, 1941. It was scarcely a month before the movie premiere and, thanks to the Warner Bros. publicity machine, York's national profile was higher than it had been in decades.

His six-foot frame now carried 275 pounds, more than 100 pounds over his fighting weight. His hair and moustache were iron gray, and reading glasses perched on his nose. He looked more like an old man than a warrior, but his message that day was supremely poignant and powerful. After thanking the Veterans of Foreign Wars for inviting him, and taking a swipe at noninterventionists "whose favorite bird must be the ostrich," he hit his stride.

There are those in our country today who ask me, "You fought to make the world safe for democracy. What did it get you?"

Let me answer them now. It got me twenty-three years of living in an America where a humble citizen from the mountains of Tennessee can participate in the same ceremonies with the president of the United States. It got me twenty-three years of living in a country where the goddess of liberty is stamped on men's hearts, as well as the coins in their pockets . . .

By our victory in the last war, we won a lease on liberty, not a deed to it. Now, after twenty-three years, Adolf Hitler tells us that lease is expiring, and after the manner of all leases, we have the privilege of renewing it, or letting it go by default. I have no doubt that the American people choose to renew it . . .

If Hitler wins in Europe, we Americans will find ourselves surrounded by hostile nations who will not, even if we choose, let us keep to ourselves. The evil combination of Germany, Italy, Russia, and Japan will then operate against us even more openly than it does now . . . [If we're willing to allow these countries to continue their aggression without a fight,] then let us stop making guns, and let us surrender to Hitler right now, while we can still do so on our own terms.

The boy whose remains are in this unknown soldier's grave wouldn't recognize that kind of an American. England is fighting for her very life—for the right of her people to be free. We have always fought for that right. If we have stopped, then we owe the memory of George Washington an apology, for if we have stopped, then he wasted his time at Valley Forge.

We are standing at a crossroads in history. The important capitals of the world in a few years will either be Berlin and Moscow, or Washington and London. I, for one, prefer Congress and Parliament to Hitler's Reichstag and Stalin's Kremlin. And because we were, for a time, side by side, I know this unknown soldier does, too.

We owe it to him to renew that lease on liberty he helped us to get.

May God help us to be equal to the task.[3]

Many Americans still disagreed that their nation should go to war. Soon after the movie premiere, Charles Lindbergh gave a speech insisting that the only people who wanted America in the fight with Hitler were "the British, the Jews, and the Roosevelt administration." Even so, he saw *Sergeant York* and liked it. "It was, of course, good propaganda for war," he wrote in his diary on September 13, 1941, "–glorification of war, etc. However, I do not think a picture of this type is at all objectionable and dangerous."[4]

The armed forces requested copies of the film to show on military bases. The night of December 6, 1941, the crew of the aircraft carrier USS *Enterprise* watched it as they sailed on maneuvers with the American Pacific Fleet. The next morning, the whole question of American intervention was rendered irrelevant after the Japanese surprise attack on Pearl Harbor. At sea when the bombing began, the *Enterprise* survived to become the most decorated ship of World War II.

The movie and the war catapulted York to national prominence. He accepted the offer of a weekly inspirational radio show. The Chicago *Sun* hired him to write a daily syndicated newspaper column for ten thousand dollars a year guaranteed (though Arthur Bushing did much of the heavy lifting for a hundred dollars a month). The first installment of "Sergeant York Says," on December 15, began, "Now the Japs have proven on our own flesh and blood that, like Hitler and Mussolini, they will stop at nothing. I had to be persuaded to fight last time. Nobody needs that today. At one blow, the Japs have welded every last American into one solid chunk of steel. They have forged the sledgehammer that will smash them."[5] York visited military bases, spoke at war bond rallies, endorsed the Red Cross, and chaired the Fentress County draft board. When the national media reported that five thousand Tennesseans had been rejected for military service because they were illiterate, and thousands more for rotten teeth, the sergeant volunteered to lead a battalion of them into combat himself, reminding reporters, "George Washington had store teeth."

Sergeant York was the highest-grossing picture of 1941 and garnered eleven Oscar nominations, winning two—Best Actor for Gary Cooper and Best Editing for editor William Holmes. York had received $50,000 in advances from Jesse Lasky by the time the movie opened. In February 1942 he received his first royalty check from Warner Bros. for $32,617.55. At year-end Alvin York had collected more than $134,000 in film royalties, more money than he had made in the rest of his life combined.

York spent his fortune almost as fast as he got it. He contributed to the cost of a gym under construction at York Institute and bought instruments for the band; supplied $38,000 toward the $40,000 cost of his new Bible school; expanded his livestock operation and set up the area's first livestock co-op; and bought a water-operated flour mill across the river from his house. On trips to New York and elsewhere, the sergeant brought back suitcases full of clothes and gifts for family and friends, including the latest fashions and expensive furs. He put the children of friends and relatives through school. He even modernized his house, adding steam radiators, two bathrooms to replace the outhouse, and running water and an electric stove in the kitchen. One of the bathrooms was converted from a closet under the stairs near the front door. This was where Alvin and Gracie had always sneaked a private good-bye kiss whenever he was leaving town. When it became a bathroom, they still slipped in as before for their farewells.

As war raged around the world, and Fentress County men left to fight again, life in Pall Mall went on much as always for those who remained. Food rationing wasn't an issue because the people raised their own; gasoline was not in demand as it was in the cities. About the only shortages folks talked about were sugar and hairpins. Sugar was important as a preservative in canning, and when cane sugar grew scarce, farmers increased their sorghum output and made sugar from that. For hairpins the ladies learned to do without or use toothpicks as a substitute.

On May 20, 1943, Mother York died quietly in her sleep at age seventy-seven. To the end she declared that Alvin was a fine boy but no finer than any of her other children. Her advice for raising good boys and girls had always been to "praise 'em some once in a while, whup 'em when they need it, and leave the rest to God."

The year 1943 marked the turning point in the war, when America went on the offensive and began taking back lost ground both in the European Theatre and in the Pacific. On July 1, President Roosevelt signed legislation instituting payroll deductions for federal income tax payments. By then Sergeant York had already had a dustup with the Treasury Department about taxes owed on his advance payment from Jesse Lasky. York had figured his 1940 tax was $473.98, but the government claimed it was $2,984. For 1941 York paid $1,137.52, but the Internal Revenue Service insisted the correct amount was $5,361.98. Under protest the sergeant paid the IRS more than $9,300 to bring his account current.[6]

The 1942 tax season brought Sergeant York a headache he would suffer with for years to come. York listed just under $6,800 in net income, plus $134,338.14 in film royalties, on which he paid more than $37,000 in taxes. The IRS insisted the correct tax amount was $91,880.69, more than $54,000 additional, assuming no penalties were assessed, plus accruing interest. By 1944, according to the government's reckoning, Sergeant York owed them in excess of $85,000. None of the tens of thousands he had spent on York Institute and the York Bible School were deductible because neither was a registered charity, and besides, the sergeant had no records of what he'd spent. He received no reimbursement or credit for time and expenses traveling to military bases and bond rallies. He had given thousands away in small amounts to family, friends, and neighbors. Now the government insisted on its tax from the film income. York had little money left and no solid records of where it all went.

In addition to his tax woes, York was enduring a rocky time with two of his sons, Alvin Jr. and Woodrow, both of whom had tended toward troublemaking since boyhood. Alvin was in prison for selling moonshine. Woodrow had been drafted and seemed to snap under the discipline. He left his training camp without permission and was brought in by military police, after which he spent time under psychological evaluation. He later escaped to Pall Mall and hid in basements in the valley for three weeks before his family discovered him. Arrested and sentenced to the military stockade, he was finally discharged after the war.[7]

Alvin York joined an exuberant, grateful nation celebrating the end of the war in the summer of 1945. Throughout the conflict *Sergeant York* had been a popular film that unflinchingly promoted traditional American values of faith, honor, and freedom. Prints dubbed into Spanish and French went to American embassies around the world, and the leader of Nationalist China, Chiang Kai-shek, requested it for his soldiers in the field. York's war with Germany and Japan was now over, but his battle with the IRS was just beginning. He and his lawyer in Jamestown, John Hale, tried to assemble the records the government insisted they had to have in order to consider reducing the amount he owed.

In the summer of 1946, York suffered a mild stroke. He refused to go to the hospital and spent a few days in bed, resuming his routine even though he felt numb on his right side. The right side of his face tingled, and sometimes he woke up at night feeling as if he were smothering. After a minor traffic accident later in the year, the numbness got worse. Still he kept a busy schedule—farming and cattle operations, visiting the Institute and Bible school, entertaining the usual noon crowd around his dinner table, and working with John Hale to try to find some way to satisfy the government's tax demands even as his energy waned and the Treasury Department debt grew every day.

OLD TIME RELIGION

For all the notoriety and riches that came his way during the 1940s, Alvin York lived much the same life he'd lived for decades. One small difference was that Gracie and the hired girls who helped in the kitchen no longer had to build wood fires in the cookstove or tote water from the well across the highway. The sergeant's stroke had slowed him a bit, and two more, one late in 1948 and another in the spring of 1949, partially paralyzed the right side of his face and left him dependent on a walking stick. After that he spent more time on his front porch or in a chair in the yard, talking eagerly with neighbors and strangers alike who stopped by to visit. He read more than he had as a young man. His office was jammed with books, and he regularly went through a stack of magazines, including news weeklies *Life* and *Look*, along with *Progressive Farmer* and *American Cattleman*.

York remained keenly interested in world events despite his

disability and advancing age, and relished any opportunity to sound off on the news of the day. He consistently supported a position of deterrence through strength, especially in dealing with the Communists. York didn't trust the Russians in Eastern Europe. "We found out what appeasement got us from Japan," he told a visitor. "If we don't stand firm, we'll have to let the atom bomb do the job. I don't think the bomb will ever be necessary, because I'm sure if we stand firm Russia will back down." Force, he said, was the only language a nation understood once it turned its back on God. The Bible, York insisted, was the only real path to world peace.

When conflict flared up on the Korean Peninsula, York advocated a strong, immediate response. "Made a bad mistake in the First World War," he said. "We should of went right on to Berlin. But we stopped, so we had another war to fight. Second War we made the same big mistake . . . So now we got another war to fight. This time I hope we don't make no mistake."[1]

As he held forth on world crises, York kept up his own skirmish with the Internal Revenue Service. John Hale and a Nashville attorney, John J. Hooker, tried unsuccessfully to work out a compromise. By the end of 1951, they were preparing to go to trial in Nashville, yet were befuddled at every turn by the lack of records. York had given away most of his fortune but had no legal proof of where it went. Hale and Hooker made and postponed the trial date several times as York struggled with the effects of his strokes, bouts of pneumonia, increasingly painful arthritis, and other ailments of advancing age. Years passed as the lawyers tried to put together a defense. Meanwhile the penalties and interest on York's liability grew every month, and the sergeant's health continued its slow decline.

On February 24, 1954, Alvin York collapsed unconscious on the floor in his farmhouse from a cerebral hemorrhage. He had shunned doctors and hospitals all his life and had been treated previously at home by his friend and physician, Dr. Guy Pinckley. This time the doctor and two of York's sons lifted him into the car for the half-day drive to Veteran's Hospital in Nashville. He was back in Pall Mall by mid-March, and there was some hope at first that he might recover. He could walk a little, giving Gracie and the family encouragement that he would get better over time. Instead, he walked less and less, until one day he didn't walk at all.

The sergeant was paralyzed from the waist down and confined to bed for the rest of his life. It didn't stop him from extending his famous hospitality. Gracie would answer a knock at the front door and find herself facing anyone from a friend down the road to a complete stranger who'd come in off the highway to a bunch of local teenagers stopping to say hello to a busload of tourists hoping to pay their respects. "Who is it, Gracie?" the sergeant would holler. Then, whatever the answer, "Tell 'em to come in!"[2]

In spite of his battle over control of York Institute, the sergeant had kept up his interest in the school and made donations even as his financial world continued to collapse. He handed out diplomas for the last time on graduation day in 1953. Still, there would be one more visit to his beloved school. He wasn't sure he could make the trip, but didn't want to disappoint all the people who came to honor him on Sergeant York Day.

It was a hot summer afternoon, August 21, 1957, when the sergeant, weak and listless, nevertheless took his place on a reviewing stand built wide enough for his wheelchair at the York Institute football field.[3] Hundreds of students, many of whose parents had also gone to the Institute, passed in review along with a forty-piece band from the 82nd Airborne Division, successor to York's All-American Division. The soldiers had flown from Fort Bragg, North Carolina, that morning to salute their famous former comrade-in-arms. The division commander, Major General John W. Bowen, declared that the 82nd "stands ready today, still inspired by the example of Sergeant York."

As the band began to play again, the guest of honor signaled that he needed to leave. General Bowen cut the festivities short and moved on to the final order of business, presenting York with the keys to a sleek, new, black-and-white Pontiac Star Chief. Its front seat had been shortened to leave space on the passenger side, and two indentions put in the right front floorboard for the sergeant's wheelchair. "I certainly thank you," York whispered. "Don't drop me, boys," he added with a grin as four soldiers transferred him to a litter, then carried him to an ambulance for the ride back to Pall Mall.

The sergeant's disability added to his lawyers' problems in trying to settle with the tax authorities. To go through with their plans for a trial, the attorneys had to get their client to the federal court in Nashville. But every time they scheduled an appearance, they had to ask for a delay because York was sick and unable to travel. At one point the government agreed to a stipulation, meaning they accepted York's version of the facts so the case could go to trial without York present. But so much time passed that there were new government lawyers in charge who refused to accept the old stipulation their own predecessors had approved.

Other public figures had worked out beneficial tax arrangements that Hale and Hooker believed York should be granted as well. Heavyweight champion Joe Louis had had more than a million dollars in tax liability erased because of his military service, when all he did was stage exhibition boxing matches and never saw combat. Former president Harry Truman had been excused from paying capital gains taxes on his memoirs, as had President Eisenhower; Hale and Hooker argued for the same treatment of York's film royalties, but the government was unconvinced.

Finally, in January 1957, the federal court told John Hooker that it would grant no more continuances. The next time, he had to present a defense or lose by default. Hooker's office wrote to York and to York's friend Dr. Pinckley, explaining that without detailed records there was nothing more they could do. Gracie was handling the sergeant's correspondence by this time, and the news petrified her. She answered Hooker with a letter begging him to help the sergeant and not to desert them. Hooker's office answered on March 26.

It is not that we do not want to help you and Sergeant York,
but there is nothing that we can do from this end of the
line . . . If you will arrange to get that detailed signed audit
and then advise us what amount of cash Sergeant York could
put up to settle the case, we will see what we can do with the
Government. Without that information our hands are tied.[4]

Tennessee senator Estes Kefauver and Congressman Joe L.
Evins appealed to the IRS on York's behalf.[5] By now York's
accrued interest was more than the original disputed tax amount.
The Treasury Department claimed that York owed $85,442 in
unpaid taxes plus $87,155 in interest since 1943, for a total past
due amount of $172,579, assuming no penalties were assessed.
At last Congressman Evins made some headway. There was
a change at the Internal Revenue Service, and the new acting
director, Charles I. Fox, was sympathetic to the sergeant's pre-
dicament. The original dispute had been over the amount of
York's taxable income in 1943. The difference between what
York said it was and the government's figure was a little over
$54,000. The tax on that difference, had York paid it that year,
would have been $29,140.80. Director Fox proposed that the
two sides settle for $29,000. When the new commissioner, Dana
Latham, took up his post, he, too, wanted to see York's problem
solved.

York by this time hadn't worked in years, his royalty
income had slowed to a relative trickle, and he was in danger of
losing the house and farm the Nashville Rotary Club had given

him more than forty years before. It looked as though if the IRS didn't take his home, other creditors might.

In the spring of 1960, York and his advisors finally cobbled together an official financial statement that showed clearly how serious the sergeant's financial straits actually were. Not only could he never pay $172,000 in back taxes; he couldn't even pay the $29,000 for a compromise settlement. His net worth was $24,813, including $20,000 equity in his farm, a Pontiac worth $750, and $2.20 in his checking account. Income for the previous year totaled $5,739.15, including about $2,600 in film royalties and $10 a month for his Medal of Honor pension.

Congressman Evins introduced two private bills on the House floor, one declaring all York's physical problems to be "service related" and therefore treated without charge by the Veterans Administration, and a second to relieve him of tax liability. Both were rejected by a House judiciary subcommittee.

Writer Inez Robb published a column about York's tax woes, commenting, "The debt the Nation owes this hero, not only for his service during the war but through the fact that his life has been a model of patriotic behavior, cannot be estimated in dollars and cents." A wave of publicity generated by the article brought a new generation of reporters, soldiers, and curious strangers to the sergeant's doorstep in Pall Mall. He talked freely to all comers about patriotism and the beauty of the Tennessee hills, and enthusiastically declared his opinion on world affairs, including the new Cuban dictator, Fidel Castro. "When are you going to take a battalion of Airborne down there and settle Castro's hash?" he wanted to know. "Next war we get into, we'd better do it with the A-bomb. And if they can't get anybody else to push the button, I will!" But the sergeant had little to say about money matters. About all the visitors could coax out of him on the subject was, "I gave the government half of [my money] and told 'em the other half was mine."

Congressman Evins doggedly pursued every avenue he could think of to find some relief for his famous constituent. He spoke with Speaker of the House Sam Rayburn and Attorney General Robert Kennedy (whose brother, incoming president John F. Kennedy, had sent York a personal invitation to the inaugural ball), and tried and failed again to introduce a bill in the House. The IRS lowered their demand again, this time to twenty-five thousand dollars, roughly equal to the sergeant's net worth.

It was Speaker Rayburn who proposed the idea of forming the Help Sergeant York Committee, a private fund-raising organization with himself as chairman. Gary Cooper made a personal donation, and Warner Bros. donated twenty-five hundred dollars. C. Douglas Dillon, secretary of the Treasury, gave a thousand dollars, as did World War I ace and president of Eastern Air Lines Eddie Rickenbacker. The challenge was getting word of the Committee out to the general public. These few high-profile gifts were a good start, but in order to meet their goal, the Committee would have to spark a generous spirit in thousands of ordinary Americans.

Sergeant York's favorite television program was *The Ed*

Sullivan Show, a variety show broadcast live by CBS every Sunday night, consistently one of the best-known and most-watched shows on the air. The Committee asked Sullivan to make an appeal for donations on York's behalf, to which the star immediately agreed. On the night of March 26, 1961, Sullivan used part of a commercial break to speak to the American people about York's financial troubles and how they could help. He concluded:

> If all of you throughout the country agree with me that this
> is a cruel, ironic, and heartbreaking thing to happen to one of
> America's greatest heroes, won't you sit down with me tonight
> after our show and send whatever small or large sum of money
> you can afford to the Sergeant York Fund, Washington, D.C.
> Never let it be said that when the chips were down for Sergeant
> York, we pulled away from him. Because certainly, with the
> chips down, he never pulled away from us.[6]

Evins had arranged with the postmaster general to send any envelopes addressed to Sergeant York in Washington to Evins's office. Within three weeks after Speaker Rayburn organized the Help Sergeant York Committee, the group banked more than $27,000, most of it in small amounts after the Sullivan broadcast. Some of the donations came with notes and letters.[7]

"From one vet to another. Wish it could be more."

"If I had money, I'd pay it all for him."

"I am a boy of 13 enclosing just one dollar. It's not much compared to what Sgt. York gave, but I hope it helps."

"Enclosed is a very, very small tribute to Sgt. York and my only apprehension is that it may pay part of someone's salary in the Internal Revenue Department."

On April 19, Congressman Joe Evins presented the IRS with a check for $25,000 on York's behalf, clearing him of all tax liability. York was delighted at the news. "I'm tickled to death to hear about this," he said from his bed in Pall Mall. "Anybody would be. You know, every time somebody makes the load of life a little lighter, it's good to hear about it."[8]

Donations continued rolling in until the surplus reached nearly $25,000. John Hooker set up a trust fund with it that would pay the sergeant and Gracie about $200 a month for the rest of their lives. Financier S. Hallock duPont, moved by York's story, set up a fund of his own with duPont stock that would yield another $300 a month. Getting wind of these gifts, the Veterans Administration canceled York's $138 monthly pension. York was humbly delighted at the two trust funds and had no comment about the VA.

Sergeant York was as ready to greet a visitor as ever, eager to talk about current events or memories of days long past. But physically he was growing weaker and more limited. He spent his days at home in a hospital bed rigged with a circular frame and an electric motor so he could tilt the mattress into a sitting position to talk with his guests. Friends took up a collection to remove his small front porch and replace it with a large, two-story veranda running across the front of the house so Gracie or one of his boys could wheel him out into the fresh air.

York and Gracie had had ten children in all, seven of whom—five boys and two girls—lived to adulthood (the last pregnancy ended in a miscarriage in 1940). When one of them got married, the newlyweds often lived at the York homestead for a while, sometimes for years, so the house was always full of family. York loved the company and the commotion. In the early 1960s the York house was as filled with life and with kinfolks as ever. In addition to York and Gracie, Gracie's sister Kansas still lived with them, as did the two youngest sons, Andrew Jackson and Thomas Jefferson, their wives, and their six children.

On December 13, 1963, Alvin York celebrated his seventy-sixth birthday with the enormous dinner that was a highlight of the year in Pall Mall. He warned the crowd that day that patriotism and faith were as important as ever, but that America was veering from the path that had brought so many years of peace and prosperity. "If this country fails," he said, "it will fail from within. I think we've just got to go back to the old time religion, shouting as though the world is on fire. Maybe people will realize we've gotten onto some wrong roads and return to the old paths."[9]

When York arrived at Veterans Hospital in Nashville in August 1964, it was his eleventh hospital stay in two years. The immediate problem was a urinary tract infection, but in truth the old veteran was simply worn out and ready to go. Gracie and their son George Edward, now a Nazarene minister, stayed in town, spending most of their time in the room with their husband and father. The sergeant had some idea that the end was near. When he and Ed were alone, the sergeant motioned his son close to ask a question that had been weighing heavy on him.

"Ed," his father whispered with effort, "do you think God has forgiven me for killing all those Germans?"

"Yes, Daddy," Ed answered through his tears. "I'm sure He has."

Soon after that, York fell into a coma. "Dad's not going home this time," Ed told his mother. "We may as well shape up for it."[10]

The morning of September 2, Gracie and Ed took a break from their vigil to get some air and exercise and drove to a large department store at the edge of downtown. Hearing themselves paged over the intercom, they went to a telephone, where a nurse told them the sergeant had died without regaining consciousness.

Three days later, on a beautiful, clear, late-summer Saturday morning, Alvin Cullum York was honored and laid to rest before a crowd of eight thousand, the largest gathering in Wolf River history. Many huddled around loudspeakers outside York Chapel to hear the funeral, while thousands more waited at the grave site across from the Methodist church, not far from Old Coonrod's resting place and only a few steps from York's son Sam Houston. President Lyndon Johnson sent Lieutenant

General Matthew B. Ridgeway, leader of the 82nd Airborne during World War II and later commander of NATO, as his personal representative. A band and honor guard from the 82nd assisted with the graveside proceedings. Six soldiers in summer khakis and spit-shined jump boots carried the casket from the church to the cemetery as the band played York's favorite hymn, "Onward Christian Soldiers."[11]

York died without a will and with a reported net worth of five thousand dollars. Gracie wanted a fitting grave marker for her husband and wrote the sergeant's old friend Lipscomb Davis, a successful banker and businessman, to ask how she might raise the money. As a college student, Davis had traveled with York on his early speaking tours. "I have had plenty of wearies since Mr. York passed away," she wrote the year after her husband died. "Oh Lipscomb I just could not tell you how much I do miss him. And of course I will always miss him as I had him to go to for advice and to comfort me until he got so sick . . . Even if he did have to stay in bed I could talk with him. But the good Lord called him away from this old world of suffering and sorrow to a world of peace and happiness where suffering will be no more."[12]

Davis went to several likely sources of funds for a grave marker, but without success. It wasn't possible to use money from the two trust funds set up on York's behalf. The governor of Tennessee, Frank Clement, said the legislature had appropriated money for a statue of York on the state capitol grounds and couldn't spend any more. The American Legion, Veterans

of Foreign Wars, and Tennessee Historical Society all declined
to assist. Gracie took out a sixty-five-hundred-dollar mortgage
on the farm and ordered the monument herself. Its two main
features were a ten-foot cross of Georgia granite and an Italian
marble statue of an angel kneeling in prayer. Next to these was
a stack of granite books that signified York's love of learning
and the inscription, "Proverbs 14:34," the sergeant's favorite
Bible verse. When Gracie escorted visitors to the site, they usually asked her what the verse was. With a smile and a twinkle in
her eye, she always replied, "Look it up."

In November 1967, the new governor, Buford Ellington,
authorized payment of five thousand dollars from the legislature's miscellaneous appropriations fund toward the note on
the York farm. Gracie was able to pay the balance and retire
the mortgage.

Mrs. York remained in the big house by the river with
Kansas, son Thomas, and his wife and two children. Thomas, a
county constable, was killed in the line of duty in 1972. Eleven
years later, Alvin Jr. died of lung cancer. Gracie continued
greeting a constant stream of strangers and well-wishers at
her front door until the end, and died quietly on September 27,
1984, at the age of eighty-four.

The York Bible School, built with such enthusiasm using
a third of the movie royalties, never got off the ground.
Completed as World War II was at its height, there were neither
teachers nor students in Pall Mall to hold classes. After the war,
York was so preoccupied with his tax woes and poor health that

he never had time to spend on it. By the mid-1950s the school was essentially abandoned and sits today, still straight and solid, in a field of weeds across the road from the old stone chimney that marks the site of Mother York's cabin.

York Agricultural Institute has a current enrollment of 650, and remained the only comprehensive high school in Tennessee funded by the state legislature until 2010, when the state provisionally passed its responsibility back to the county school board. The four-hundred-acre campus (reported to be the largest high school campus in the world) includes a working farm and a park. The school received a National Blue Ribbon of Excellence in 1989, and in 1992 *Redbook* magazine designated York Institute one of the best rural schools in America.

The original brick building in which York took such pride still stands, but was replaced in 1981 by modern classrooms next door that were air-conditioned and that met updated fire safety regulations. Almost ever since, the old structure has been the subject of a debate over whether to tear it down or restore it. In 2009 the state turned the building, along with five hundred thousand dollars budgeted for its demolition, over to the nonprofit Sergeant York Patriotic Foundation, which hopes to preserve it. The sergeant's three surviving children, George Edward Buxton, Andrew Jackson, and Betsy Ross, maintain a keen interest in the school, the historic building, and their father's legacy.

That legacy has dimmed over time. When Sergeant Alvin York came home to a hero's welcome in 1919, his was the biggest ticker-tape parade in New York history up to that time. Day after day his name appeared in the *New York Times*. He was an international celebrity. Today most Americans younger than fifty have never heard of him. Yet the example he set is a powerful and compelling one. York's faith transformed his life, and that transformation in turn had a ripple effect that eventually touched millions.

York often talked about how poorly educated he was. Certainly he was no intellectual or theologian. His Christian faith was uncomplicated, almost childlike, and yet it was complete and all-sufficient. The spiritual journey of this humble backwoods farmer took him into the presence of prime ministers and presidents. It made him a household name for two generations. And his life is still a reminder that the power of faith can equip even the meekest and most modest of us for a great work that we scarcely dare to dream of.

NOTES

CHAPTER 1

1. John Perry, *Sgt. York: His Life, Legend & Legacy: The Remarkable Untold Story of Sgt. Alvin C. York* (Nashville: Broadman & Holman, 1997), 39.

CHAPTER 2

1. Alvin Cullum York and Thomas John Skeyhill, ed., *Sergeant York: His Own Life Story and War Diary* (Garden City: Doubleday, Doran and Company, Inc., 1928), 145.
2. Perry, *Sgt. York*. See pages 41ff. for the full account of the revival.
3. York and Skeyhill, *Sergeant York*, 149.
4. Ibid., 153ff. for all of York's correspondence with the draft board.

CHAPTER 3

1. York and Skeyhill, *Sergeant York*, 164ff. for all war diary quotations. The diary is also available online at *http://acacia.pair.com/Acacia. Vignettes/The.Diary.of.Alvin.York.html#The%20Diary*.
2. Ibid., 169–73 for York's account of his discussion with Danforth and Buxton.
3. Ibid., 175–176.
4. Perry, *Sgt. York*, 75–77.

CHAPTER 4

1. Perry, *Sgt. York*, 77. York's letters to Gracie from France are in the library archives at Tennessee Technological University, Cookeville, Tennessee.
2. Ibid.
3. The account of York's battle for Hill 223 is taken from official reports and eyewitness affidavits collected years later by Warner Bros. screenwriters working on the film script. These documents are at the Warner Bros. Film Archive on the campus of the University of Southern California–Los Angeles. Quotations from York within the account are from the war diary in York and Skeyhill, *Sergeant York*.

Chapter 5

1. This postcard remains with a descendant of the recipient, whom the author thanks for sharing it.
2. Perry, *Sgt. York*, 91.
3. The Medal of Honor citation and presentation comments are in the Warner Bros. archive.
4. War diary, quoted in York and Skeyhill, *Sergeant York*, 295.

Chapter 6

1. All of Chase's quotations and the account of his work are from Joseph Cummings Chase, "Corporal York, General Pershing, and Others," *World's Work*, April 1919, 636–48.
2. All of Pattullo's quotations and the account of his work are from George Pattullo, "The Second Elder Gives Battle," *Saturday Evening Post*, April 26, 1919, 1ff.
3. The account of York's New York reception appears in his war diary in York and Skeyhill, *Sergeant York*, 295–302. The New York celebration, York's homecoming, and his marriage are detailed in numerous articles in the *New York Times*, particularly the following (all for the year 1919, page numbers and column numbers in parenthesis): March 22 (6:2); May 24 (12:7); May 25 (14:3); May 26 (10:2); May 27 (7:3); May 30 (7:1); June 1 (section 2, 1:6); June 8 (13:3); June 11 (3:6); June 12 (18:5).
4. Perry, *Sgt. York*, 115.

Chapter 7

1. The account of York's wedding is compiled from *Times* articles listed in chapter 6, note 3; local contemporary sources quoted in Perry, *Sgt. York*, 116–30; and an author interview with Billy Conatser of Pall Mall, whose ancestors attended the wedding and reception and had passed down to him their eyewitness report. Billy also led the author on a tour of the wedding site, unmarked and now completely overgrown.
2. All quotations during the wedding celebration regarding York profiting from his fame are from "What Shall It Profit a Man? Says Sgt. York" in the Nashville *Tennessean* (June 8, 1919).
3. Perry, *Sgt. York*, 128.
4. Ibid., 130.
5. "Honor Read and York," *New York Times*, July 13, 1919, 8:2.

6. Perry, *Sgt. York*, 142.
7. Ibid.
8. Details of York's fund-raising trips are compiled from the Tennessee Tech archives, letters loaned to the author by the York family, and letters loaned by Mrs. Dorothy Bushing, daughter-in-law of York's business secretary, Arthur Bushing.
9. Perry, *Sgt. York*, 144, 145.
10. Ibid.

CHAPTER 8

1. Gracie's letters here are in the archive at Tennessee Tech, quoted in Perry, *Sgt. York*, 153–54.
2. Author interview with York's son George Edward.
3. Letter loaned to the author by the York family.
4. Deed is on file at the Fentress County Courthouse, Jamestown, Tennessee.
5. Perry, *Sgt. York*, 169.
6. Ibid., 171.
7. Ibid., 172.
8. Ibid.

CHAPTER 9

1. Details of York's lecture tours are from his letters home to Arthur Bushing and Gracie, and from local news accounts. Letters are compiled from the York collection at Tennessee Tech, family members who loaned their private letters to the author, and Mrs. Dorothy Bushing.
2. See York and Skeyhill, *Sergeant York*, 5ff. for accounts of Skeyhill's visits to Pall Mall.
3. Details of Skeyhill's business arrangements are in letters between him and York in the Tennessee Tech archives.
4. The account of Sam Houston's death was given to the author by Sam's older brother, George Edward York.
5. Telegram from the York papers at Tennessee Tech, quoted in Perry, *Sgt. York*, 222–23.
6. Perry, *Sgt. York*, 227.
7. Ibid., 228–29.

CHAPTER 10

1. Jesse L. Lasky's story and quotations throughout come from his autobiography, *I Blow My Own Horn* (Garden City: Doubleday & Co., 1957).

2. All information about the film production, including intrigue surrounding the loan of Gary Cooper, is from office memos, screenwriting files, and daily shooting reports in the Warner Bros. archives.

CHAPTER 11

1. Accounts of the film premieres in New York and Washington are from the Warner Bros. archives, and from media reports quoted in Perry, *Sgt. York*, 265–72.
2. An account of meeting President Roosevelt was graciously provided to the author by one who was there, young Arthur Bushing.
3. "What Did It Get You?" *Time*, June 9, 1941.
4. Charles A. Lindbergh, *The Wartime Journals of Charles A. Lindbergh* (New York: Harcourt Brace Jovanovich, Inc., 1970).
5. Alvin York, Sergeant York Says, *Tennessean* (Nashville), December 15, 1941.
6. Details of York's tax problems are from the Tennessee Tech letters and financial reports in the Warner Bros. archives.
7. The accounts of Alvin Jr. and Woodrow are from author interviews with their siblings George Edward York, Andrew York, and Betsy Ross York Lowery.

CHAPTER 12

1. York's comments on current affairs are from Perry, *Sgt. York*, 296–97.
2. Account of York's years as an invalid kindly supplied to the author by family members.
3. Account of Sergeant York Day from Jim Scott, "Courageous York Forced to Leave Jamestown Fete," *Nashville Banner*, August 22, 1957, 10.
4. York letters collection, Tennessee Tech.
5. Details of York's IRS dealings are from letters at Tennessee Tech.
6. *The Ed Sullivan Show*, Sofa Entertainment, March 26, 1961.
7. Donor letters all from Tennessee Tech.
8. James Talley, "'I'm Mighty Grateful' says Sergeant York," *Tennessean*, March 19, 1961, 16.
9. Perry, *Sgt. York*, 319.
10. This account of York's last days from an author interview with his son George Edward.
11. "Sergeant York, War Hero, Dies," *New York Times*, September 3, 1964, 1.
12. Letter loaned to author by the York family.

BIBLIOGRAPHY

"Calls Sergeant York 'Bravest of Men.'" *New York Times*. March 22, 1919, 6:2.

Chase, Joseph Cummings. "Corporal York, General Pershing, and Others." *World's Work*. April 1919, 636–48.

Cowan, Sam. *Sergeant York and His People*. New York: Funk & Wagnalls, 1922.

The Ed Sullivan Show. Sofa Entertainment. March 26, 1961.

Fentress County Public Records. Jamestown, Tennessee.

Glaenzer, B. "The Ballad of Redhead's Day." *New York Times*. May 24, 1919, 16:2.

"Honor Read and York." *New York Times*. July 13, 1919, 8:2.

Lasky, Jesse L., and Don Weldon. *I Blow My Own Horn*. Garden City, NY: Doubleday & Co., 1957.

Lindbergh, Charles A. *The Wartime Journals of Charles A. Lindbergh*. New York: Harcourt Brace Jovanovich, Inc., 1970.

"Nashville Honors York." *New York Times*. June 11, 1919, 3:6.

"Offers Commission to York." *New York Times*. May 30, 1919, 7:1.

Pattullo, George. "The Second Elder Gives Battle." *Saturday Evening Post*, April 26, 1919, 1ff.

Perry, John. *Sgt. York: His Life, Legend & Legacy*. Nashville: Broadman & Holman, 1997.

Scott, Jim. "Courageous York Forced to Leave Jamestown Fete." *Nashville Banner*. August 22, 1957, 10.

"Sergeant York Home, His Girl Says, 'Yes.'" *New York Times*. June 1, 1919, sec. 2, 1:6.

"Sergeant York Is Feted." *New York Times*. May 26, 1919, 10:2.

"Sergeant York Marries Boyhood Sweetheart." *New York Times*. June 8, 1919.

"Sergeant York, War Hero, Dies." *New York Times*. September 3, 1964, 1.

Skeyhill, Tom. *Sergeant York: Last of the Long Hunters*. Philadelphia: John C. Winston, 1930.

York, Alvin. Sergeant York Says. *Tennessean*. December 15, 1941.

York, Alvin Cullum, and Skeyhill, Thomas John, ed. *Sergeant York: His Own Life Story and War Diary*. Garden City: Doubleday, Doran and Company, Inc., 1928.

Talley, James. "'I'm Mighty Grateful' says Sergeant York." *Tennessean*. March 19, 1961, 16A.

Tennessee State Library and Archives, John Trotwood Papers.

————— Small collection. Letters (to Sgt. Alvin York) 1939–1943.

————— Tennessee Historical Society Speeches.

————— Vertical File, Alvin C. York.

Warner Bros. Film Archives, University of Southern California Library, Los Angeles.

"Washington Hails Brave Sergeant York." *New York Times*. May 25, 1919, 14:3.

"What Shall It Profit a Man? says Sgt. York." *Tennessean*. June 8, 1919.

"What Did It Get You?" *Time*. June 9, 1941, Vol. XXXVII No. 21.

"York Gives Up Honeymoon." *New York Times*. June 12, 1919, 18:5.

"York Sees Subway from Private Car." *New York Times*. May 27, 1919, 7:3.

ACKNOWLEDGMENTS

O f the many people who have so graciously and patiently answered my questions about Sergeant York, I owe special debt to his children George Edward Buxton York, Andrew Jackson York, and Betsy Ross York Lowery, who have spent countless hours with me and shared countless excellent meals. Thanks also to Mrs. Dorothy Bushing, whose husband, the late Dr. Arthur Bushing, was the son of York's business associate Arthur Bushing, and who recently loaned a newly discovered trove of York letters. I'm grateful as well to Lipscomb Davis Jr., whose father accompanied York on some of his early speaking trips, and who has worked tirelessly to keep the Sergeant York Patriotic Foundation on solid ground.

This book would have been impossible without the help and guidance of Kristen Parrish and Joel Miller at Thomas Nelson, and the wise counsel of my agent and friend Andrew Wolgemuth. Thank you all. I've done my best to give the sergeant the story he deserves.

ABOUT THE AUTHOR

John Perry was born in Kentucky and grew up in Houston, Texas. He attended University College, Oxford, England, and graduated *cum laude* from Vanderbilt University in Nashville. John has appeared on C-SPAN *Book TV*, *The Janet Parshall Show*, *The G. Gordon Liddy Show*, and other syndicated broadcast shows. He has published biographies of Charles Colson, Gov. Mike Huckabee, Booker T. Washington, George Washington Carver, Mary Custis (Mrs. Robert E.) Lee, and Sergeant York. His coauthored novel, *Letters to God*, is a *New York Times* Best Seller. John lives in Nashville, Tennessee.

Close Encounters of the Christian Kind

— Available Now —

SAINT NICHOLAS
9781595551153

D. L. MOODY
9781595550477

WINSTON CHURCHILL
9781595553065

JANE AUSTEN (9781595553027)
ANNE BRADSTREET (9781595551092)
WILLIAM F. BUCKLEY (9781595550651)
ISAAC NEWTON (9781595553034)

SAINT FRANCIS (9781595551078)
SAINT PATRICK (9781595553058)
JOHN BUNYAN (9781595553041)

Available April 2011

GALILEO
9781595550316

ALBERT SCHWEITZER
9781595550798

JOHANN SEBASTIAN BACH
9781595551085